MODERN EGYPT

WHAT EVERYONE NEEDS TO KNOW®

MODERN EGYPT

WHAT EVERYONE NEEDS TO KNOW®

BRUCE K. RUTHERFORD
JEANNIE L. SOWERS

OXFORD
UNIVERSITY PRESS

OXFORD
UNIVERSITY PRESS

Oxford University Press is a department of the University of Oxford. It furthers
the University's objective of excellence in research, scholarship, and education
by publishing worldwide. Oxford is a registered trade mark of Oxford University
Press in the UK and certain other countries.

"What Everyone Needs to Know" is a registered trademark of
Oxford University Press.

Published in the United States of America by Oxford University Press
198 Madison Avenue, New York, NY 10016, United States of America.

© Oxford University Press 2019

Library of Congress Cataloging-in-Publication Data
Names: Rutherford, Bruce K., author. | Sowers, Jeannie Lynn, 1967– author.
Title: Modern Egypt : what everyone needs to know /
Bruce K. Rutherford, Jeannie L. Sowers.
Other titles: What everyone needs to know.
Description: New York, NY : Oxford University Press, 2019. |
Series: What everyone needs to know
Identifiers: LCCN 2018018996 | ISBN 9780190641146 (hardcover : alk. paper) |
ISBN 9780190641153 (pbk. : alk. paper)
Subjects: LCSH: Egypt—History—2011– | Egypt—History. |
Egypt—Geography.= | Egypt—Economic conditions—21st century. |
Egypt—Religion. | Egypt—Foreign relations—21st century.
Classification: LCC DT107.87.R88 2019 | DDC 962.05—dc23
LC record available at https://lccn.loc.gov/2018018996

1 3 5 7 9 8 6 4 2
Paperback printed by Sheridan Books, Inc., United States of America
Hardback printed by Bridgeport National Bindery, Inc., United States of America

CONTENTS

3 Building a New Regime: Nasser, Sadat, and Mubarak   46

4 Economic Development and Human Welfare   77

5 Environmental Issues, Natural Resources, and Quality of Life   101

6 Religion   121

7 Foreign Affairs   140

PREFACE: WHY STUDY EGYPT?

The Middle East is in the midst of extraordinary turmoil. In 2011, a wave of popular uprisings threatened authoritarian regimes that had held power for decades. Mass demonstrations in Tunisia, Egypt, and Yemen, combined with militaries unwilling or unable to repress them, forced long-standing autocrats from power. Yet subsequent political developments diverged widely in these countries. Only Tunisia emerged with a more open political system, which remains fragile in the face of economic challenges, social polarization, and the war next door in Libya. Egypt, as we explore in this book, developed a deeper authoritarianism with a more central role for the military in politics and the economy. Yemen was caught in a devastating cycle of civil and regional conflict that produced a humanitarian catastrophe. Regimes in Syria, Libya, and Bahrain responded to popular uprisings in their countries with brutal force, which radicalized some of their opponents and invited external interventions. With devastating civil wars and intensified inter-state conflict across much of the region, the heady days of revolutionary protest in 2011 and 2012 seem a distant memory.

As this turmoil unfolded, Egypt's 2011 uprising and its aftermath played an especially important role. Egypt's size and historical importance make it one of the most influential countries in the region. It has the largest population of any Arab country (95 million; the next largest, Sudan, has 40 million) as well as the Arab world's largest army and third-largest economy. The country commands a strategic location at the geographic heart of the Arab world and controls the Suez Canal, one of the region's most important waterways. Egypt also exerts substantial soft power. Its renowned al-Azhar University is the premier center of Islamic study and teaching in the Sunni world. Egyptian artists and writers shape the culture of the region at all levels, from pop music and soap operas to abstract art. The country also sends many thousands of teachers, engineers, and doctors to work in surrounding states, adding another dimension to its reach and impact. In addition, Egypt has served as a model for political development in other Arab states. Its political and legal institutions have been emulated to varying degrees in Kuwait, United Arab Emirates, Jordan, Iraq, and Syria.

Studying modern Egypt is thus essential to understanding the region's future. If Egypt can come to grips with its many problems and create a more stable and just order, the prospects for the region are substantially brighter. In contrast, if it goes the way of Libya or Syria, the region will be mired in an ever-deeper cycle of poverty and violence that could last for generations.

The purpose of this book is to introduce nonspecialists to this important and influential country. We have each studied Egypt for more than 20 years and have engaged in extensive language study and field research in the country. We have learned an extraordinary amount from our Egyptian colleagues, many of whom stood on the front lines of the 2011 uprising and have risked their lives in pursuit of a better future. We have also benefited from the many excellent scholarly works in Arabic and English on the country's history, politics, economy, and culture.

However, the remarkable richness of the literature on Egypt is somewhat of a curse for anyone who endeavors to write a short book. In a volume of only 200 pages, we inevitably made difficult choices about material to leave out. The brevity of our analysis of some topics by no means suggests that they are unimportant. Rather, we have focused our discussion on key events, actors, institutions, and issues that are essential for gaining a basic knowledge of Egypt. We hope to achieve two goals: to leave the reader with a sufficient appreciation of Egypt to understand its current challenges and opportunities, and to spark the reader's interest in this fascinating country. We hope that readers will be inspired to read more of the vibrant scholarship on Egypt that has proven such a valuable resource for us.

We begin the volume by discussing the historic uprising that captured the world's attention in January and February 2011. In order to understand this event, we introduce several important themes—the role of the military and internal security agencies in politics and the economy; the characteristics of Egyptian authoritarianism under Mubarak; the political role of Islam and, particularly, the Muslim Brotherhood; the weakness of Egyptian political parties and civil society groups; and the deep structural problems of the Egyptian economy that have led to extensive poverty and substantial inequality. These themes are then developed in subsequent chapters. Chapters 2 and 3 deal with the central features of Egyptian history, with particular attention to the changes undertaken since Gamal Abdel Nasser's rise to power in 1952. Chapter 4 examines several critical issues in human development and welfare including population growth, inequality, unemployment, urbanization, and the status of women. Chapter 5 introduces readers to important environmental and natural resource issues, including pollution, climate change, and fossil fuel dependency. Chapter 6 discusses the major religious communities and actors. Chapter 7 considers Egypt's foreign policy and its position within the regional and international order. Chapter 8 examines the country's current and future challenges and its strategies for addressing them.

The authors would like to thank the anonymous reviewer for many helpful suggestions and David McBride, our editor at Oxford, for his assistance throughout the process. We are grateful to Michelle Woodward, who found the photographs for the book, and to our respective institutions for their generous support to pay for the photos: the College of Liberal Arts at the University of New Hampshire and The Research Council at Colgate University. We are also grateful to our research assistants: Hayley Lazzari, who did a fine job of reading the entire manuscript and offering suggestions; and Matt Goduto for his research and formatting assistance. Jeannie L. Sowers would like to thank John Waterbury for motivating her to study Egypt in the first place.

Small portions of Chapters 2, 3, 6, and 7 utilize material from Rutherford's *Egypt after Mubarak* (Princeton, 2008) and his "Egypt's New Authoritarianism under al-Sisi" (*Middle East Journal*, Spring 2018). This material is used with permission.

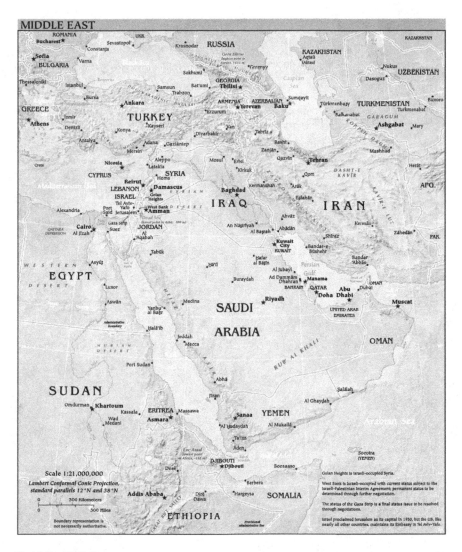

Map 1 The Middle East

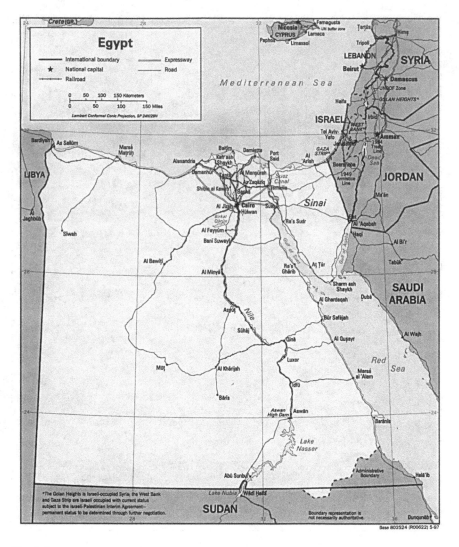

Map 2 Egypt

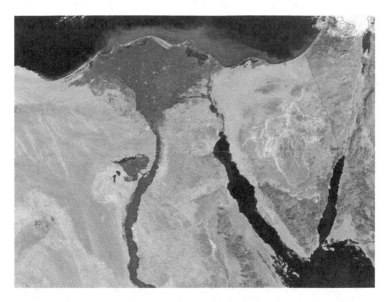

Map 3 NASA satellite image of Egypt, including Nile Delta and Sinai Peninsula

Map 4 NASA satellite image of Egypt at night, showing urbanization, dense settlement pattern, and electrification

MODERN EGYPT

WHAT EVERYONE NEEDS TO KNOW®

1

THE 2011 UPRISING AND ITS AFTERMATH

What Happened on January 25, 2011?

Egyptian activists called for street protests against the long-standing rule of President Hosni Mubarak on January 25, 2011 using a variety of social media platforms including Facebook, Twitter, and YouTube. They chose January 25 because it is National Police Day, a countrywide holiday originally established to commemorate the bravery of 50 Egyptian policemen killed in a clash with British troops in January 1952. To the surprise of the organizers, approximately 20,000 people gathered in Tahrir Square in downtown Cairo, marking the largest protest in years. Large street demonstrations also took place in the provincial cities of Alexandria, Mansoura, Sohag, Minya, Suez, El-Arish, Luxor, Aswan, Asyut, Tanta, and others. In Suez, four young men were killed in confrontations between the police and protesters. In response, Suez residents torched the local police station, attacked police vehicles and checkpoints, and marched on the headquarters of President Mubarak's National Democratic Party. With these dramatic events, the "January 25 revolution," as Egyptian activists termed it, was underway.

Over the next 18 days, police, hired thugs, and protesters confronted each other across the country. Internal security forces deployed tear gas, water hoses, batons, and birdshot to disperse the protests. The violent response by security forces only increased resistance as youth leaders organized another nationwide demonstration on January 28, termed the "Friday of Rage." Hoping to disrupt the protests, the Mubarak government cut phone and internet connections, but to no avail. In Cairo, demonstrators gathered in several neighborhoods after Friday prayers and then moved toward Tahrir along the city's major thoroughfares and bridges. Marchers encouraged onlookers to join them through rhymed chants in Egyptian Arabic, such as "Why are you watching from far away? You're Egyptian, aren't you?" and "Raise. Raise the voice. He who chants will never die."[1] People left their homes and workplaces and poured into the streets, or cheered the marchers from their balconies. The Ultras, soccer fans known for their violent confrontations with security forces, joined in, as did the youth wing of the Muslim Brotherhood and Egyptians from all walks of life. On Cairo's Qasr al-Nil Bridge, thousands of people pushed forward against police lines, water cannon, and tear gas volleys to triumphantly reach Tahrir Square, where an estimated 80,000 people assembled. Volunteers set up tents, makeshift hospitals, and stages for campaigners to make speeches and lead songs, while food and drink vendors circulated among the crowd. Activists set up improvised barricades to protect themselves from the security forces, broke up sidewalks and pavement for projectiles, and established volunteer brigades to vet those entering the sit-in.[2]

Across the country, protesters clashed with the Central Security Forces (CSF) and police on the Friday of Rage and in the ensuing days. An estimated 84 to 150 police stations were attacked, as well as state security offices, police checkpoints, and police vehicles.[3] As the police faltered, the regime increasingly relied on hired thugs and loyalists. In the famous "Battle of the Camel," on February 2, a group of thugs riding horses and camels attacked the Tahrir sit-in while pro-Mubarak marchers entered the square. Eleven people were killed and 600 wounded, but the anti-Mubarak protesters held Tahrir.

The police and CSF proved incapable of handling what rapidly became a countrywide revolt. Overwhelmed and demoralized, they simply withdrew from the streets. The regime was forced to deploy the military and declare a curfew in Cairo, Suez, and Alexandria. In Tahrir, the protesters threw roses at the tanks that were deployed around the square, chanting "the military and the people are one hand," trying to ensure that the troops would not fire.

President Mubarak's televised speeches announcing relatively small concessions were too little and too late. Much of the public viewed his performances as patronizing, out of touch, and dismissive of the mass movement and its martyrs. Strikes and other labor actions by industrial workers, lawyers, doctors, textile workers, and others spread throughout the country, intensifying the pressure on the military leadership to take action.

After 18 days of confrontation and chaos, the military leadership removed Mubarak. They announced that they would rule directly, as the Supreme Council of the Armed Forces (SCAF), until parliamentary and presidential elections could be held. In Tahrir and across the country, protesters celebrated. Fireworks, music, and a heady festival atmosphere ensued as Egyptians in the squares and streets enthusiastically debated the contours of a new order long into the night.[4]

The military's decision to facilitate Mubarak's removal came as a surprise to many. Like all of Egypt's presidents, Mubarak hailed from the military. He was the commander of the air force in the early 1970s before Sadat appointed him vice president in 1975. Mubarak was thus well aware of the importance of maintaining strong ties with the military leadership and directly appointed all of the senior officer corps. However, by the time of the 2011 uprising, the generals concluded that he had become a liability. They had reportedly grown disenchanted with Mubarak's increased reliance on the internal security forces under the Ministry of Interior, which consumed resources that could have gone to the military. They may have also believed that Mubarak was grooming his son Gamal to succeed him, particularly after Gamal was appointed to one of the highest positions in the regime's ruling National Democratic Party. Gamal was widely viewed as a prominent beneficiary of the extensive corruption that plagued the Mubarak era, using his political status to accrue a large fortune. In addition, the military reportedly feared that Gamal favored economic reforms that might jeopardize their business interests, which include dozens of firms involved in construction, farming, tourism, and other fields.[5]

What Factors Triggered the 2011 Uprising?

Egyptians have suffered from unemployment, poverty, and an abusive security state for decades. However, several factors coalesced in the late 2000s that made them more willing to take to the streets despite the risks. These included escalating police abuse, a rapid rise in prices of food and other necessities, and the stunning example of the successful uprising in Tunisia.

Human rights abuses by Egypt's security forces have been a long-standing problem. These abuses intensified in the 1990s, as the regime engaged in an increasingly brutal clash with Islamist opponents primarily in the southern part of the country. The security forces frequently employed collective punishment, arbitrary detention, sexual humiliation, and torture. In the 2000s, these tactics spread more widely and were adopted by police throughout the country in their daily interactions with citizens. It became increasingly common for average Egyptians from the middle and lower classes to face police abuse, leading to growing public anger.[6]

A particular act of police abuse against Khaled Said, a young businessman, focused this anger and helped bring many ordinary Egyptians into the streets in January 2011. On June 6, 2010, Said died in police custody from a beating he received from two plainclothes policemen in broad daylight outside an internet café in Alexandria. Photos circulated online of his battered and disfigured body. The attempt by the police to discredit him as an alleged drug dealer further catalyzed public anger. A Facebook page titled *"Kullina Khaled Said"* ("We are all Khaled Said") quickly attracted 400,000 members. On January 14, 2011, the administrator of the page—Wael Ghonim, a Google executive working in Dubai—invited Egyptians to take to the streets on January 25, 2011. His invitation and the efforts of many other activists helped to produce large crowds in Tahrir Square and elsewhere in Egypt.[7]

Economic hardship also played a role in the uprising. The 2008 global economic crisis effected many Egyptians as prices for virtually all the country's imports rose dramatically. In particular, Egypt relies on imports of rice and wheat to cover the needs of its population. The prices for these grains rose especially sharply due to crop failures in several major exporting countries including Russia and India. The increasing cost of food and other essentials pushed many Egyptians into poverty. By the time of the uprising in 2011, two-thirds of Egyptians— some 55 million people—were eligible for subsidized food items from the government based on their low incomes. In 2011, over 20 percent of Egyptians lived on 1 US dollar or less per day.

Egypt's middle class—meaning those with some high school or university education— also faced economic difficulties in the years before the uprising. Their real wages declined even as the country's overall economic output grew, in part due to rising inflation. Educated graduates faced dwindling job prospects and fading opportunities for a better life. For the vast majority of middle class youth, earning a high school or university degree did not lead to upward mobility or increased income.[8] The declining fortunes of educated young people helps to explain why so many of them took to the streets in the 2011 uprising.[9]

While police abuse and economic conditions intensified dissatisfaction with Mubarak's regime, the mass demonstrations in Tunisia against long-standing ruler Zine El Abidine Ben Ali in December 2010 persuaded many Egyptians that the time had come to act. These demonstrations were trigged by an incident in a small rural town in Tunisia, Sidi Bouzid. On December 17, 2010, a police officer in the town confiscated the produce of a street vendor named Muhammad Bouazzizi. The officer also seized his cart, making it impossible for him to make a living. As an act of protest, Bouazzizi set himself on fire in front of the town's municipal building a few hours later. He eventually died from his burns. As with Khaled Said's death at the hands of Egyptian police, many Tunisians viewed the police harassment and humiliation of Bouazzizi as emblematic of the routine abuse suffered by ordinary citizens under President Ben Ali. Demonstrations against Ben Ali began throughout the country and steadily grew, despite the best efforts of Tunisia's security police. When the military chose not to intervene to defend Ben Ali, he fled to Saudi Arabia. To ensure that the post–Ben Ali government was not simply stacked with old regime stalwarts, demonstrations continued and workers and professionals conducted a series of general strikes. Footage of these dramatic events in Tunisia circulated widely on the internet as well as on international media outlets such as the satellite TV station al-Jazeera. Egyptians thus had a front row seat to the fall of Ben Ali on January 14, 2011 and its aftermath.

Tunisia shares several important similarities with Egypt. Both countries have long histories of strong labor movements, university activism, and street mobilization. Unemployment and underemployment among semi-educated and educated youth is extensive. Wealth is concentrated in the capital and coastal regions, with the interior and rural areas left behind. If a popular uprising could force the fall of an autocratic government in Tunisia, why not in Egypt?

Who Were the Protesters and What Did They Want?

The protests were organized by loose networks of young activists that included students, veterans of pro-democracy and human rights groups, women's rights activists, urban intellectuals, middle class professionals, leftists, Nasserists, and youth groups from the Muslim Brotherhood. In Alexandria, Suez, and other cities with large state-owned industrial areas, public sector workers also staged demonstrations and strikes. From the Islamist camp, the mainstream cadres of the Muslim Brotherhood participated, although the more conservative Salafi movement largely remained on the sidelines.

Many of the activists who coordinated the 2011 protests had prior experience organizing demonstrations. Young activists and veteran organizers had staged pro-democracy and antiwar protests on campuses, outside embassies, and in major squares during the 2000s. They demonstrated against the US-led Iraq war in 2003, the Mubarak regime in 2005, Israel's war in Lebanon with Hizballah in 2006, and Israel's war in Gaza with Hamas in late 2008 and early 2009. In 2005, the pro-democracy movement "Kifaya!" or "Enough" embodied the frustration of many Egyptians with the Mubarak regime's performance on both economic and foreign policy. In 2008, the April 6 movement organized street protests to support striking textile workers in the Delta city of Mahalla al-Kubra. Although strikes were outlawed under Egypt's emergency laws, workers staged hundreds of unauthorized labor actions throughout the 2000s, as did civil servants, public sector employees, and middle class professionals. During the 2000s, the security forces were able to contain demonstrations and strikes. In 2011, however, the broad diffusion of protest across most of Egypt's cities overwhelmed the state's security apparatus.[10]

For many activists, removing Mubarak was the first step toward deeper changes to the political system. The popular slogan of all the Arab uprisings, "the people want the fall of the regime," highlights these broader goals of economic and political transformation. Their aims included electing a new legislature with broader jurisdiction; scrapping the emergency laws that granted the President enormous powers; adopting a new constitution to protect civil and political rights and constrain the executive; strengthening judicial independence and the rule of law; reforming the security services; and electing governors and city officials rather than filling these posts through presidential appointments. The activists also had socioeconomic demands, including a minimum national wage, the recognition of independent unions by the government, an end to corruption and crony capitalism, and the renationalization of public sector industries that many felt had been sold to private businessmen at bargain prices.

Partly in response to these demands, the public prosecutor initiated corruption cases against several prominent businessmen associated with the Mubarak regime such as the steel tycoon Ahmad Ezz. Yet these small victories became less frequent as activists found themselves confronted by better-organized conservative forces. These included the security apparatus, which largely disappeared off the streets

Photo 1.1 Egyptians read the latest news as they gather to protest the Mubarak government on the "Day of Martyrs," which honored those killed in the clashes in Tahrir Square. February 6, 2011.

Credit: Ron Haviv / VII / Redux

but remained intact; the military; and what activists dismissively termed the *fulul*, the remnants of the old regime. While activists participated in many political forums, parties, and social projects that emerged after Mubarak's removal, they lacked the organizational clout to give their demands traction and to offset the power of these conservative forces.

The defenders of the old order commanded substantial political machines at the local level. In addition, the military elite did not split into moderate and hard-line factions, in which moderates might have joined the activists to support deeper reforms. Instead, the generals remained unified and defended the old system of economic and political administration that they knew well. They did not reform the security agencies and judicial system, as the protesters demanded. As the transition unfolded, the revolutionary activists were increasingly marginalized and eventually subject to extensive repression under successive post-2011 governments.

Did Large Uprisings Occur before 2011?

Egyptians participated in several large-scale protests during the twentieth century. In 1919, Britain sent the Egyptian nationalist leader Saad Zaghloul into exile, sparking a countrywide uprising that heralded the beginning of the end of direct British colonial rule. In January 1952, as noted previously, British forces killed 50 Egyptian policemen in the Suez Canal city of Ismailiyya, leading to demonstrations across Cairo that set the stage for a military coup a few months later that ended the Egyptian monarchy and British colonial influence.

In 1977, mass protests erupted across Egyptian cities when then-president Anwar Sadat announced cuts in state subsidies for basic food items such as wheat flour and cooking oil. The riots began in the port city of Alexandria, known for its labor and leftist movements, and then spread to Cairo, Helwan, Suez, and other cities. Protesters targeted the private residences of Sadat and then–vice president Hosni Mubarak as well as nightclubs, fancy cars, and other symbols of elite wealth. The internal security forces were unable to restore order, and Sadat was forced to call in the military and impose citywide curfews. Calm was restored when Sadat formally rescinded the price increases. Over the course of a few days 80 Egyptians were killed and 800 injured.

The Central Security Forces (CSF), which are the regime's first line of defense against protests, are also a potential source of unrest. Upwards of 25,000 CSF personnel rioted in 1986 on hearing rumors that their conscription term would be extended from three to four years. Mubarak had to call on the Egyptian military to put down the mutiny.

These past uprisings share several features with the 2011 uprising. High prices and other economic grievances helped send ordinary people to the streets despite the country's extensive security forces. Egypt's provincial cities as well as the capital Cairo served as centers of revolt. In addition, the military intervened to direct the course of political events. The military leadership viewed itself as the protector of the Egyptian nation against both external meddling and internal disorder.

How Did the Supreme Council of the Armed Forces Govern after the 2011 Uprising?

Once Mubarak was deposed, 20 senior generals, known as the Supreme Council of the Armed Forces (SCAF), assumed control of the country until Egypt's first post-Mubarak presidential elections were held. During their sixteen months in power, the military leadership saw their primary tasks as demobilizing the streets, restoring stability, and reviving the economy. The SCAF engaged in substantial repression of the popular forces behind the uprising even as it invoked the revolutionary rhetoric of patriotism, nationalism, and populism.

Pro-democracy activists organized large street demonstrations in major cities during the months after Mubarak's removal, keeping pressure on the SCAF for reform. In early March 2011, the SCAF was forced to dismiss the prime minister appointed by Mubarak to control the uprising, Ahmad Shafiq, and his cabinet. The new cabinet appointed by the SCAF included several well-known technocrats and academics sympathetic to reform.[11] The SCAF was also pressured to abolish the Ministry of Information, while the new Minister of Interior formally dissolved the regime's internal surveillance agency, although it would soon re-emerge in full force after the 2013 military coup.

These gains came against the backdrop of the military's increasing use of lethal force against unarmed protesters. In what could be viewed as a dress rehearsal for their later repression of the Muslim Brotherhood in 2013, the military abandoned its neutral stance toward protesters. Military police and the central security forces attacked sit-ins and protests. Their tactics included the infamous "virginity tests" administered by the military against female activists during a protest in Tahrir Square on March 9, 2011; attacks on a protest march against military rule near SCAF headquarters on July 23; and the use of tanks and other heavy vehicles to kill 24 people and leave 300 wounded in an attack on activists who were protesting the persecution of Coptic Christians. On December 16, 2011 the military also dispersed a sit-in outside the interim prime minister's office. This action left an estimated 13 dead and included the stripping and beating of an unarmed female activist, which was caught on film and broadcast widely. Alongside the increase in violence against civilians, the military depicted protesters as provocateurs, thugs, criminals, and foreign agents.

In addition, many activists became worried about the growing cooperation between the SCAF and the Muslim Brotherhood in 2011/2012. Once Mubarak was deposed, the bulk of the Brotherhood withdrew from street protests. Adapting their slogan "Islam is the solution," leading Brothers argued that "elections are the solution," not street protest.

They believed that the Brotherhood's extensive grassroots organization would give it a significant advantage in elections, and focused their efforts on persuading the SCAF to allow elections as quickly as possible. The Brotherhood's decision to engage with the SCAF broke the 2011 revolutionary coalition and reduced pressures for substantive institutional reform.

Why Did the Muslim Brotherhood Win Egypt's First Post-Mubarak Elections?

Egypt's first free parliamentary elections in over 60 years were held between November 2011 and January 2012. Candidates running under the umbrella of the Muslim Brotherhood won 42 percent of the seats in the Majlis al-Shaab, the lower house of Parliament, and 58 percent of the contested seats in the Majlis al-Shura, the upper house.

The Brotherhood had been in existence since 1928, with local-level networks resilient enough to withstand intense repression in the 1950s and 1960s. After the 2011 uprising, the Brotherhood created a political party—the Freedom and Justice Party (FJP)—that drew on the organization's extensive grassroots base and its tight organizational hierarchy. The FJP competed in every electoral district in the parliamentary elections. Its candidates often had deep roots in their communities and long-standing ties with local religious institutions. In contrast, the more secular revolutionary activists were dispersed among more than 25 political parties in the months following Mubarak's ouster. Most of these parties were led by political novices with no prior experience contesting elections and little political or financial organization to support their candidates.[12]

Voters proved willing to give the Brotherhood a chance after decades of single-party rule under the government's National Democratic Party. However, analysis of polling data makes clear that this support was not a blank check nor was it an endorsement of the Brotherhood's plans to expand the role of

Islam in public life. Rather, voters expected the Brotherhood to deliver on its promises to improve state services and broaden economic opportunity.[13]

A similar pattern emerged in the 2012 presidential election. Just as the FJP offered a clear and unified alternative to a large number of small liberal parties, the Brotherhood's Muhammad Mursi won the 2012 presidential election because several centrist candidates split much of the vote in the first round of the presidential election. In this first round, four serious contenders emerged in addition to the Brotherhood's Muhammad Mursi: Ahmad Shafiq, a senior figure from the Mubarak regime; Hamdeen al-Sabahi, representing leftist and Nasserist currents; Abdel Moneim Abu al-Fatouh, a former Brotherhood leader expelled from the organization for insubordination; and Amr Moussa, a former minister of foreign affairs and the former head of the Arab League. Al-Sabahi, Abdel Fatouh, and Moussa were widely considered the centrist candidates. They collectively won the largest share of votes—49.3 percent—but these votes were split among them. As a consequence, Mursi and Shafiq moved on to the final round of the presidential election with vote shares of only 24.8 percent and 23.7 percent, respectively. Egyptians thus faced a difficult choice: side with Shafiq, whom many believed would roll back the achievements of the 2011 uprising and restore the old regime; or take a chance on Muhammad Mursi, who had called for a more democratic political system and a more prosperous economy. By only 4 percent, voters chose Mursi.

Despite this narrow margin, Mursi and his supporters interpreted the outcome as an endorsement of the Brotherhood's leadership and goals. This misreading of the electoral result emboldened the Brotherhood to attempt to govern without building coalitions with other political forces. This proved a fatal mistake. One year after taking office, Mursi would be overthrown in a military coup amidst mass popular demonstrations.

Why Were President Mursi and the Muslim Brotherhood Forced from Power in 2013?

The Brotherhood had great difficulty making the transition from opposition to governing, while state authorities did little to help them and may have actively hindered them by creating shortages in basic goods and keeping police off the streets. In addition, youth activists and others involved in the 2011 uprising became increasingly concerned that the Brotherhood was excluding them from decision-making. These fears were seemingly confirmed when Mursi issued a presidential decree in November 2012 that placed his decisions beyond review by the Constitutional Court, which Mursi felt was stacked with judges determined to sabotage him. For many Egyptians, this step signaled that the Brotherhood would act in a unilateral and authoritarian manner. Many Egyptians were also worried about the emerging priorities of the Brotherhood. While the Brotherhood leadership had softened its rhetoric and expressed its support for a civil state grounded in democratic principles, the Brotherhood's local campaigns and electioneering raised doubts about the organization's commitment to the rights of women, the protection of minorities, and the defense of secular law. Liberals, women, and Coptic Christians, as well as many Muslims, feared that the Brotherhood would seek to "Islamize" state institutions and public culture in a less tolerant direction.

In addition, the economic situation during Mursi's tenure continued to deteriorate. Although the government issued ambitious plans for developing the economy, it was unable to work effectively with state agencies to implement them. Inflation continued to rise, partly due to the declining value of Egypt's currency, while tourism income and foreign direct investment remained weak. Mursi's government continued negotiations with the International Monetary Fund for a large loan to tide the government over while it embarked on structural economic reforms. It also increased short-term government spending on subsidies and public wages in a bid to lessen the impact of the worsening economic situation. In 2013, the government spent roughly 33 percent of total government expenditure on subsidies, an amount equal to roughly 13 percent of GDP.[14]

The country's economic problems were compounded by the fact that the Brotherhood's leaders lacked the political skills to govern effectively. They had spent their adult lives in conflict with the state, facing the constant threat of arrest and imprisonment. As a result, they had built a closed organization in which secrecy and suspicion of outsiders were essential for survival. They mistrusted Egypt's bureaucracy and the officials who led it, as well as the popular forces that had spearheaded the uprising.

This mindset led the Brotherhood's leaders to adopt an increasingly exclusionary approach to governing, which was particularly evident during the drafting of a new Constitution. Under the legal framework in place at the time of Mursi's election, the Parliament was empowered to select an assembly to draft a new Constitution. At that point in time, only the upper house of Parliament was still seated, where the Brotherhood held a majority. Thus, the Brotherhood had a decisive voice in choosing delegates to the constitutional assembly. To the disappointment of the 2011 activists, the Brotherhood's leaders appointed roughly 70 percent Islamists to the constitutional assembly and provided little representation to women, Copts, or liberals. These minorities became increasingly frustrated by their inability to influence constitutional discussions. Many of their delegates in the constitutional assembly resigned in protest. The Brotherhood's leaders in Parliament replaced them with more Islamists, further aggravating fears that the Brotherhood's rhetoric of inclusion was hollow.

At the same time, the Constitutional Court indicated that it was likely to rule that the constitutional assembly should be disbanded. Mursi and the Brotherhood had tangled previously with the Constitutional Court, whose judges were appointed under Mubarak. This Court had dissolved the Brotherhood-controlled lower house of Parliament on the eve of Mursi's election in June 2012, in what many believed was an effort to block the Brotherhood from controlling both the executive and the legislature. Faced with the prospect of the Constitutional Court dissolving the constitutional assembly as well, Mursi took a fateful step. As mentioned earlier, he issued a presidential decree in November 2012 that placed his decisions beyond the reach of the Constitutional Court's review and, thus, insulated the constitutional assembly from any threat of dissolution. Supporters of Mursi observed that this decree would be operative for only three weeks, until the new Constitution was submitted to a public referendum. However, this subtlety was lost in the ensuing melee, as many secular and liberal activists saw Mursi's decree as a rejection of democratic principles and an attempt to create a new autocracy. Opponents of the decree and of the Brotherhood-led government organized large demonstrations in Tahrir Square and outside the presidential palace. These demonstrations led to clashes between supporters and opponents of Mursi that killed at least 10 people.[15] Liberal activists urged Egyptians to vote no on the new Constitution. To their disappointment, voters approved it by 64 percent in the December 2012 referendum. This episode permanently divided the liberal revolutionary coalition from the Brotherhood.

During its time in power, the Brotherhood cooperated with the military in a variety of ways. The 2012 Constitution written by the Brotherhood-dominated assembly preserved the privileges of the military and granted it greater autonomy than it enjoyed under previous constitutions. Mursi was also careful not to touch the military's budget or the authority of the senior military leadership to decide how it was spent. Mursi also made clear that the Brotherhood would not seek to undue the peace treaty with Israel, which was of paramount concern to the military, the United States, and Israel.

The military's leaders, however, became alarmed with the Mursi administration's approach to several important foreign policy issues. In a sharp break with Mubarak-era policies, Mursi attempted to improve relations with Iran. Mursi visited Iran and invited Iran's then-president Mahmoud Ahmadinejad to visit Cairo. He also publicly declared his support for the Palestinian group Hamas, which had been established in Gaza in 1987 as a local offshoot of the Brotherhood. Many in Egypt's security apparatus were wary of Hamas and considered it a terrorist group. Mursi further aggravated these fears when he invited an individual convicted of involvement in Anwar Sadat's assassination to participate in an official commemoration of the 1973 war. In addition, in June 2013, Mursi called for "foreign intervention" in the conflict in Syria in order to protect that country's Sunni population. Some Egyptian military leaders were reportedly concerned that Mursi intended to send Egyptian combat forces to Syria or was encouraging Egyptian volunteers to fight on the side of armed Sunni radical groups. Finally, members of Egypt's elite expressed concern about Mursi's ability to safeguard the country's access to the waters of the Nile. In 2012, Ethiopia was building a large dam, the Grand Ethiopian Renaissance Dam, on the upper reaches of the Nile. Mursi seemed uncertain how to respond. An Egyptian TV broadcast of supposedly secret meetings of Mursi and his cabinet included his advisors threatening Ethiopia with military action, which further embarrassed Mursi's government.

Mursi's popularity and that of the Brotherhood also declined because of an increase in crime and shortages of electricity and fuel. The Brotherhood was unable to control either the public utilities that distribute gasoline and electricity or the Ministry of Interior that supervises the police. Many middle- and lower-level bureaucrats, particularly those in the security agencies, were deeply suspicious of the Brotherhood and its motives. It appears that the Ministry of Interior and state-owned energy companies arranged for shortages of electricity, gasoline, and policemen in the streets, which fueled popular discontent with the Brotherhood.[16] After Mursi's removal in July 2013, gasoline and electricity became readily available and police suddenly reappeared on the streets to manage traffic and patrol neighborhoods.[17]

All of these factors combined to spark popular mobilization against Mursi. An opposition group called *Tamarrod* ("rebellion") began collecting signatures on a petition demanding that Mursi resign and that new presidential elections be held immediately. The organization also called for anti-Mursi demonstrations on June 30, 2013, the first anniversary of his election as president. Many Egyptians joined Tamarrod because of the grievances mentioned above. In addition, the Egyptian security services reportedly provided some funding, logistics, and organizational support to the movement.[18] The army and police made clear that they would not protect the Brotherhood's Freedom and Justice Party (FJP) offices from attack, and the police did not intervene—with one exception—when 47 FJP offices around Egypt were attacked and burned in late June and early July of 2013.[19] Security forces may also have participated in these attacks. The sense of crisis was further heightened when leading army officials warned of civil war and deployed the army around public facilities and protest sites.[20] President Mursi responded with defiant speeches proclaiming that he was the legitimate president of the country and that he and his supporters would fight to protect his legitimate government from "counter-revolutionaries."[21]

The June 30, 2013, public demonstrations against the Brotherhood across Egypt were the largest since the uprising of 2011. As the demonstrations continued, the military intervened on July 3, 2013 and removed Mursi, suspended the Constitution, and appointed a prominent judge as interim president. Mursi was subsequently charged with corruption, treason, murder, and abuse of power. He remains imprisoned along with thousands of other members of the Brotherhood.

How Did the Muslim Brotherhood Respond to Its Removal from Power?

The Brotherhood's leadership declared Mursi's removal an act of betrayal that violated the Constitution. They claimed that deeply entrenched centers of power within the military and the bureaucracy had engineered the failure of his government as well as his removal from office. They called on all Egyptians to go to the streets in protest. Anti-coup protesters occupied two large squares in Cairo—Rabaa al-Adawiyya and al-Nahda—as well as public spaces in major cities across Egypt. On August 14, the military and police attacked protesters at the Raba'a and al-Nahda square sit-ins, killing between 800 and 1,000 civilians. Human Rights Watch observed that the attack was "perhaps the largest mass killing of protesters on a single day in modern history, worse even than Tiananmen Square."[22] Abdel Fatah al-Sisi's government also declared the Brotherhood a terrorist organization and imprisoned thousands of its supporters, confiscated businesses owned by its members, dissolved more than 500 Brotherhood-affiliated nongovernmental organizations (NGOs), and outlawed the group's political party, newspaper, radio station, and television station.

While state repression intensified dramatically, protests against the coup continued. Protesters tried a variety of tactics to evade state security forces. As the Brotherhood's leaders were arrested and imprisoned, local anti-coup groups sprang up. Because gathering in major squares during the day made them an easy target, Brotherhood supporters staged short "butterfly" sit-ins and human chains that would appear in squares and road intersections and then quickly dissipate before security forces arrived. Protests also shifted to smaller, residential streets and to the early morning and late evening hours. While these changes in tactics allowed protests to be sustained in the face of lethal repression, the number of protests declined and they were less visible to the general public.[23]

Photo 1.2 Supporters of deposed Egyptian President Muhammad Mursi during their sit-in at Rabaa al-Adawiyya square, Cairo. July 17, 2013.
Credit: Asmaa Waguih / Reuters

The crackdown sparked an intense debate within the Brotherhood over how to survive and pursue its goals. Those who advocated for peaceful and incremental change through participation in politics had been discredited in the eyes of some members. In this view, the Brotherhood participated peacefully in politics and society from the mid-1970s through mid-2013 played by the rules, and won control of Parliament and the presidency through successful competition in elections after 2011. It was then rewarded with a coup and brutal suppression. Nonetheless, despite this painful history, the senior leadership of the Brotherhood continues to oppose the use of violence. However, the regime's crackdown on the Brotherhood weakened the disciplined chain of command that enabled the leadership to enforce its views on members. Some younger members regard their elders as timid and out of touch with the pain inflicted on the rank and file. There is some evidence that individual members of the Brotherhood have participated in attacks on police and security forces, but the Brotherhood's leadership and organization have not adopted a strategy of terrorism in order to achieve their goals.

What Are Some Features of President Al-Sisi's Regime?

When Abdel Fatah al-Sisi and the military took power on July 3, 2013, they suspended the Constitution and called for new parliamentary and presidential elections, much as the SCAF had done in 2011. Al-Sisi had spent his career in the military and was widely seen as a protégé of Mubarak's long-serving Minister of Defense, Hussein Tantawi. Tantawi appointed al-Sisi director of military intelligence in 2010, where he had the opportunity to build personal relationships with Egypt's key allies and their militaries. Tantawi was forced to step down as Defense Minister in August 2012, following an attack on Egyptian soldiers in Sinai by radical Islamists that killed over 16 men. President Mursi quickly appointed al-Sisi to replace him.

A few months after the removal of Mursi, al-Sisi announced that he would run for president in May 2014. State-owned media outlets began a barrage of pro-Sisi publicity and old regime elites saw an opening to regroup in the electoral arena. Only one candidate dared to run against al-Sisi, the leftist Hamdeen al-Sabahi, who had also run in 2012. Voter turnout was significantly lower than in 2012, and the government extended voting for an additional day in the hope of getting more voters to the polls. It also threatened to fine voters who did not participate. Amid charges of electoral manipulation and vote rigging, al-Sisi won with 96 percent of the vote.

Al-Sisi faced re-election in March 2018. Several possible challengers, including former chief of the general staff of the armed forces Sami Anan and former prime minister under Mubarak Ahmad Shafiq, were blocked from running or pressured to withdraw. The government also arrested the former head of the Central Auditing Organization and Anan's vice presidential choice, Hisham Geneina, who had publicly claimed that corruption was still rampant. Al-Sisi faced only one opponent, Moussa Mustafa Moussa, who adopted the unusual campaign strategy of repeatedly expressing his support for al-Sisi. The regime undertook an extensive get-out-the-vote campaign that reportedly included promises of food, public services, and cash. Al-Sisi won with 97 percent of the vote.[24]

Since al-Sisi's rise to power in 2013, the regime has closed off virtually every peaceful avenue for the expression of dissent. Parliament has become largely a cheerleader for the government. The regime has disbanded hundreds of civil society groups with even distant ties to political Islam. A new law regulating NGOs adopted in May 2017 further restricts the capacity of civil society groups to organize and to advocate for change. The government has frozen the accounts of human rights and development organizations that receive funding from overseas and, in several cases, arrested the directors and staff of human rights groups on the grounds that they are agents of foreign powers. The regime has also taken a harsh stance toward public protest. A new protest law, adopted in 2013, requires that protesters receive advance approval from the judiciary. Any protest without this approval is dispersed quickly and, often, violently. In addition, anyone who disagrees with regime policies can face stiff penalties. For example, a new counterterrorism law defines terrorism as the "use of force or violence or threat" that aims to "disrupt general order" or "harm national unity." This very broad definition—which includes even a perceived threat—means that virtually any act of dissent can be construed as terrorism and quickly prosecuted in a specialized court.

Al-Sisi's regime has substantially strengthened the security apparatus. The Ministry of Interior (MOI) has increased in size and has returned to acting with impunity, engaging in abuses of average citizens and torture of detainees. In addition, the military has assumed a more prominent role in domestic security. Several new laws empower the military to protect state-owned land and infrastructure and to disperse demonstrations on any street, bridge, or square. Military courts are authorized to try civilians deemed threatening to national security. In addition, hundreds of activists and Islamists have been "disappeared" or detained in secret detention sites.[25]

Egypt's security apparatus is also engaged in direct conflict with several armed groups. These groups emerged particularly in Sinai, where the Egyptian army had limited numbers of troops due to a clause in the 1979 peace treaty with Israel that demilitarized the peninsula. Ansar Beit al-Maqdis (now called Sinai Province) and other radical groups have attacked police facilities, army personnel, security checkpoints, and tourists. Sinai Province took responsibility for several major attacks including the downing of a Russian passenger plane in southern Sinai in 2015. Political violence tied to Sinai Province reached Cairo in 2015, with the assassination of the general public prosecutor and the bombing of the Italian consulate. Sinai Province attacked a Sufi mosque in Sinai and killed over three hundred worshippers in 2017. It also claimed responsibility for a mortar attack on a military airport in northern Sinai in a failed attempt to assassinate the Minister of Defense and Minister of Interior. In addition, it has conducted a brutal campaign against Egypt's Coptic Christian community that has killed or wounded hundreds of people.

In response, the Egyptian military has escalated its campaign against Sinai Province. As discussed in Chapter 6, Egypt's counterinsurgency efforts have met with only limited success, in part because the military's tactics have killed or wounded many civilians. These tactics have deepened local resentment of the military and of the government in Cairo.

What Economic Challenges Does Al-Sisi's Regime Face and How Has It Responded?

Political and economic instability after 2011 led to rising unemployment as tourism dried up, foreign investors pulled out, and wealthy Egyptians sent their money overseas. The country was also faced with mounting domestic debt and sustained downward pressure on the exchange rate. The Egyptian central bank's attempts to prop up the exchange rate by buying Egyptian pounds drained the country's foreign exchange reserves, leaving enough to cover only a few months' worth of essential imports. The country's deteriorating economy was the overriding concern of most Egyptians. When the 2014 Arab Barometer public opinion survey asked about the most important challenges facing Egypt, 88 percent of Egyptians surveyed reported "the economic situation (poverty, unemployment, and price increases)," with the second highest concern listed as corruption. Only 1.3 percent reported "achieving stability and internal security" as the most pressing problem, the theme most emphasized by the al-Sisi government.

Faced with mounting economic crises, all of the post-2011 governments negotiated with the International Monetary Fund (IMF) for large loans in return for undertaking economic reforms designed to restore investor confidence, improve credit ratings, and address pressing budget and trade deficits. In 2016, the al-Sisi government finally reached an agreement with the IMF for a three-year, US$12 billion loan, to be disbursed incrementally as the country undertook specific policy reforms. These included floating the Egyptian pound, raising central bank interest rates to curb inflation, reducing energy subsidies, and introducing a new value-added tax (VAT).

These short-term austerity measures created significant hardship for ordinary Egyptians. Floating the pound resulted in the currency losing almost half of its value, which contributed to inflation reaching over 30 percent in April 2017. Cuts in government subsidies for fuel hit many Egyptians hard, particularly those in poor households. At the national level, accepting loans from the IMF and several Persian Gulf states increased levels of external debt. External debt as a percentage of Egypt's gross domestic product (GDP) rose from 15.1 percent in 2013 under Mursi to 33.6 percent in 2016–17. At the same time, total public sector debt—that is, debts owned by state entities to both private and public agencies—amounted to 91.1 percent of Egypt's total GDP.[26] Maintaining the payments on these debts will be a continuing challenge for Egypt's economy.

The al-Sisi government also announced several large infrastructure projects that were intended to stimulate growth. The government promised to build 1 million units of low income housing at a total cost of US$20 billion, construct a new administrative capital east of Cairo at an estimated cost of US$45 billion, and complete an enormous Mubarak-era development project in the southwestern desert (called Toshka) aimed at relocating population to the area. The government further initiated a regional development project for the Suez Canal area that includes expansion of six Egyptian ports, construction of six tunnels underneath the Suez Canal, and the dredging of a parallel canal to allow more ship traffic, at an estimated cost of over US$55 billion.

Egypt has attempted similar "mega-projects" in the past, with mixed results. These projects are often burdened by cost overruns, corruption, and overly optimistic projections of future revenue. They rarely attract new economic investment or generate many jobs. This has been the case with the Toshka project, and the Suez Canal project already shows signs of these problems.[27] In an effort to capture the public's imagination, al-Sisi prioritized dredging the new parallel canal in only one year. This tight schedule required hiring foreign firms with specialized dredging equipment at a significant premium, greatly increasing the cost of the project.[28] In addition, it is not clear whether these costs will be recouped through increased shipping traffic and higher transit tolls. Similarly, while upgrading the ports and transportation system of the entire Suez Canal area could support new manufacturing and service activities, it remains uncertain whether private or public investors will choose to invest in light of the country's economic, political, and security challenges. Critics argue that the huge sums allocated to this project could have been spent more productively on smaller-scale infrastructure projects as well as measures to improve health and education.

Egypt also faces the prospect that inflation, a weak currency, and cuts in universal subsidies will further impoverish the country's many poor families. Egyptian authorities have not released updated poverty statistics, but in 2012/2013 the government reported that over one-quarter of the population—approximately 21.7 million people—were unable to meet their basic needs.[29] As mentioned earlier, perceptions of rising economic inequality contributed to the public anger that fueled the uprising in 2011. Al-Sisi has not implemented a clear strategy for managing the near-term hardships and inequality produced by reform. As we explore in subsequent chapters, the political challenges of fundamental economic reforms will prove as formidable for al-Sisi as they did for his predecessors.

Suggested Readings

The Journey to Tahrir: Revolution, Protest, and Social Change in Egypt
(Verso, 2012) compiles articles by leading scholars of Egypt originally published in *Middle East Report*. Their essays cover economic, cultural, and political developments in the last decade of the Mubarak regime and during the 2011 uprising. Neil Ketchley's *Egypt in a Time of Revolution: Contentious Politics and the Arab Spring* (Cambridge University Press, 2017) provides a detailed account of the dynamics of political protest from 2011 to 2014. For another careful study of the protests in 2011, see Kira D. Jumet, *Contesting the Repressive State: Why Ordinary Egyptians Protested during the Arab Spring* (Oxford, 2017). Gilbert Achar offers an insightful overview of the regional uprisings until 2013 in *The People Want: A Radical Exploration of the Arab Uprisings* (University of California Press, 2013). Several excellent memoirs of the uprising have appeared in English, including the novelist Ahdaf Soueif's *Cairo: Memoir of a City Transformed* (Anchor Books, 2012).

2

THE RISE OF MODERN EGYPT

How Has Geography Shaped Egypt?

A quick glance at a satellite photo of Egypt reveals the country's unusual geography: a narrow strip of green along the Nile River fanning into a verdant river delta, surrounded on both sides by vast deserts. Ninety-five percent of Egypt's territory is desert. Its 95 million citizens live almost entirely along the Nile Valley and Nile Delta.

Egypt's geography has several important repercussions for society and politics. In the country's early history, the large deserts to the east and west served as deterrents to invading armies. In addition, the dangerous rapids of the Nile just south of Aswan (near the current border with Sudan) made incursions from the south difficult, while the Mediterranean granted protection from threatening forces to the north. These conditions supported the emergence of a vibrant civilization, which enjoyed substantial security due to its geographic isolation and extraordinary wealth from the fertility of soils flooded regularly by the Nile. This isolation, security, and wealth help to explain the uniqueness of pharaonic culture as well as its extraordinary architectural and artistic achievements. They also produced a distinctive Egyptian identity that persists to the present day.

In addition, the country's geography facilitated the development of central government. The Nile's annual floods were a mixed blessing for Egyptians. They brought essential silt that restored the productivity of the soil, but they also swept away property and lives. Central administrative institutions emerged as early as 3100 B.C.E. This early state, led by pharaohs who claimed divine origin, established monitoring stations along the full length of the river that informed those living downstream about the likely timing and size of the annual floods. The state also constructed and managed irrigation canals and, later, dams that reduced the destructiveness of large floods and ensured sufficient water to support at least one crop per year and, possibly, two. In addition, the central government stored seeds that it distributed to farmers and stockpiled grain to feed them and their families during lean years when the flood was low. As the Egyptian state grew, the country's geography was, again, an asset. The concentration of the population within a relatively small area facilitated the collection of taxes and made the suppression of uprisings easier.

Egypt is one of the driest countries in the world. Annual rainfall in the wettest portion of the country (along the Mediterranean coast) is only 7 inches. The arid central and southern parts of the country receive little or no rain. Egypt's water supply comes almost entirely from the Nile, which means that Egyptians take an enormous interest in developments upstream that affect the river's flow. The Nile begins its journey in Rwanda and passes through six other countries on its way to Egypt—Burundi, Tanzania, Kenya, Ethiopia, Uganda, and Sudan. During the height of the British Empire in the late nineteenth century, Britain controlled or influenced most of these countries and used its position to issue decrees that reserved the lion's share of Nile water for Egypt. Britain's policy on Nile water was grounded in its self-interest. Egypt was an essential producer of crops, particularly cotton, which supported Britain's textile mills and industrial production. British officials were thus eager to ensure that Egyptian farmers had access to ample water.

However, as the twentieth century unfolded, newly independent upstream nations wanted to harness the Nile's waters to support their own development. Egypt followed these proposals with enormous concern. It used its influence in international institutions to slow efforts to construct dams in Ethiopia and Kenya. However, Ethiopia—with the assistance of China—began building a massive dam on the headwaters of the Nile in 2011. As discussed in Chapter 7, Egyptian officials responded with vague threats of military action and economic sanctions as well as ongoing negotiations over management of the river's waters.

Finally, Egypt is located at the crossroads of three continents: Africa, Asia, and Europe. The ruler who controls Egypt can project influence in each of these arenas. As a consequence, Egypt has attracted the attention of great powers for centuries and has endured extensive foreign involvement in its affairs including Greek and Roman invasions in ancient times, Ottoman invasions in the Middle Ages, and a British invasion in the late nineteenth century. This strategic importance was further enhanced with the opening of the Suez Canal in 1869, which provided a link between the Mediterranean and the Red Sea that enabled much quicker transit for ships between Europe and Asia. The British invasion of Egypt in 1882 was motivated, in part, by its desire to ensure access to the Canal.

What Are the Most Important Legacies of the Empires That Ruled Egypt Prior to the Start of the Modern Era in 1805?

Most historians date the emergence of modern Egypt to 1805, when an Ottoman officer named Muhammad Ali became the leader of the country and adopted wide-ranging reforms that helped to create a modern state and economy. However, Egypt had an extraordinarily rich history prior to this date. King Narmer unified Upper Egypt (the southern part of the country) and Lower Egypt (the northern part) into a single kingdom in 3100 B.C.E. Native-born pharaohs ruled until 332 B.C.E. When the Greeks under Alexander the Great invaded in that year, they began a long history of foreign control over Egypt that would last more than two millennia—until Gamal Abdel Nasser's coup in 1952.

Egypt was an important center of culture and science under the Greeks, when the great library of Alexandria flourished and leading scholars such as Archimedes and Euclid walked its halls. The Romans came next, borrowing freely from pharaonic institutions and symbols to legitimate several dynasties that made Egypt the breadbasket of the Roman Empire. Rome fell in the fifth century C.E. and the center of the Christian world shifted eastward to Constantinople (modern Istanbul), the capital of the Byzantine Empire. Egypt became a commercial hub for the Byzantines as well as a center for the development of Christian doctrine in the early centuries of Christianity. The Arab invasion in the seventh century brought Islam to the country. The first Islamic empire in Egypt, the Fatimids, had its roots among North African Berber Muslims who practiced Shia Islam. The Fatimids were succeeded by the Sunni Ayyubids, who built Cairo into a major trading center that connected the Arabian Peninsula, the Eastern Mediterranean, and Europe. The Mamluks came next and ruled for close to three centuries. They were master horsemen and archers recruited from the Caucasus (north of the Caspian Sea) who initially served as slaves and soldiers for Egypt's rulers, but later came to rule the country. The Mamluks presided over the expansion of Egyptian influence throughout the territories of modern-day Israel, Palestine, Jordan, Syria, and Turkey.

The Ottomans swept into Egypt in 1517 and remained for 281 years. Among their many contributions, they created Egypt's first standing army, which provided protection for the caravans that supported the country's economy. The most important caravans transported Muslims to Arabia for the pilgrimages each year and carried Egypt's yearly tribute to the

Ottoman capital in Istanbul. The rank and file of the military that the Ottomans built was staffed almost entirely by native-born Egyptians. Egyptians also held positions throughout the civil administration. Thus the Ottomans, perhaps unintentionally, created a class of Egyptians with the skills and experience to protect the country and to manage the economy and bureaucracy.

The Ottoman system of taxation (*iltizam*) entailed auctioning off the rights to utilize a piece of agricultural land to the highest bidder. The winner was responsible for maintaining order on the land, supervising its agricultural production, collecting taxes, and delivering a share of these taxes to the local government in Cairo. By the eighteenth century, these tax farmers were permitted to pass the land that they controlled to their heirs, effectively creating a landholding class that controlled ever-larger portions of the country's territory. The Ottomans also expanded Cairo's role as a trading center in the Eastern Mediterranean with a particular focus on the new trade in coffee, which was one of the most lucrative products of the age. Beans grown in Yemen were transported to Cairo and then sold throughout the Empire as well as Europe, leading to enormous incomes for the coffee traders and their patrons. The term "mocha" appeared in English by 1733, meaning fine coffee, and is derived from the Yemeni port city of Mokha on the Red Sea.

The Ottoman era came to an end in 1798, when Napoleon invaded Egypt in an effort to expand France's influence in the Eastern Mediterranean and to disrupt Britain's transportation routes to India. France's control did not extend far beyond Alexandria and Cairo and its stay in Egypt was a tale of woe. The French fleet was destroyed by the British toward the end of 1798. A French expeditionary force in Palestine was defeated by Ottoman troops and further decimated by disease. One year after arriving, Napoleon left the country and returned to France to organize the coup that would bring him to power. The French withdrew all of their forces in 1801.

Who Was Muhammad Ali? What Was His Impact on Egypt?

Amid the instability that followed the French withdrawal in 1801, the Ottoman Sultan sent two battalions of troops to restore order. One of these consisted of Albanian soldiers whose second-in-command was Muhammad Ali. When the leader of the unit died, Ali assumed command and promptly realized that his forces had sufficient strength to subdue both local Mamluk militias and other Ottoman forces. He declared himself Khedive and promised to resume Egypt's annual payment of tribute to the Sultan. The Sultan agreed, and the ambitious soldier became the unchallenged leader of the Ottoman Empire's most populous and prosperous territory.

As befitted his military background, Ali was acutely concerned with Egypt's military strength. The memory of the ease with which French forces had sliced through Egyptian territory was fresh. He also feared possible interventions by the British or the Ottomans. In addition, he was eager to build his wealth by expanding the country's economic and military reach. A stronger military would make Egypt both more secure and more prosperous. In the wake of Napoleon's final defeat in 1815, many French military officers found themselves unemployed and were willing to serve as advisors and trainers in other countries. Ali took full advantage of their skills and hired many Frenchmen to train Egyptian soldiers in newly established schools for the artillery, infantry, and navy. He appointed foreigners to the most senior ranks in the military, but allowed native-born Egyptians to populate the lower officer ranks and virtually all of the rank and file positions.

Ali also recognized that a modern military needed a modern economy to equip and feed the army and to generate the tax revenue to pay for it. He invested heavily in new irrigation projects and introduced new export crops, such as high-quality long staple cotton that was prized by textile factories in Britain and France. He undertook an extensive industrialization campaign that included factories to produce weapons, ammunition, textiles, refined sugar, and other products. In order to acquire the capital for these projects, the state's role in the economy expanded dramatically. The state took control of most agricultural land. The government also became the sole purchaser of raw materials as well as the sole distributor of goods of all types, enabling it to add taxes and fees at every step in the production and distribution chain. Ali created an extensive bureaucracy to manage these many tasks, which became the foundation for the modern Egyptian state. Most of these new civil servants were native Egyptians.

Ali further realized that a modern economy required a modern education system. He sent Egypt's most talented students to study in Austria, France, and Italy. They were required to return home to teach the next generation and to translate European works on virtually every topic into Arabic. He also opened new schools that utilized European curricula and taught secular subjects such as natural sciences, medicine, engineering, law, literature, and art.

Ali used his new military strength to broaden Egypt's economic and political influence. His army defeated Ottoman forces on several occasions and gained control of the Hijaz (in Western Arabia), Palestine, Syria, and southern Anatolia to within 100 miles of Istanbul. This military prowess was of obvious concern to the Ottomans. The British also feared that Ali could threaten their interests through his control over essential raw materials and trade routes. Britain sent troops to support Ottoman forces fighting Ali's army in Lebanon, while the British navy sank most of Egypt's ships in a clash off the coast of Greece. Ali had little choice but to accept an accord with Britain in 1840 that limited the size of his military. This agreement also stipulated that the state's dominance of the Egyptian economy, including the government's monopoly over raw materials and distribution networks, must end in order to "facilitate free trade." Ali's system of tariffs designed to protect Egypt's infant industries was also removed, again in the name of facilitating trade. Some state lands were transferred back to large landholding families, reviving the landowning class that emerged under the Ottomans. Egypt's economy began to focus on producing agricultural goods for export, particularly cotton for Britain's textile factories.

By the end of Ali's reign in 1847, Egypt's infrastructure had grown dramatically. In addition to improved irrigation, the country had a much more extensive network of roads, bridges, and ports. This infrastructure was designed to facilitate the production of agricultural goods (particularly cotton, sugar cane, and wheat) and the transportation of these goods for export. The Egyptian economy developed meaningfully under Muhammad Ali, but it was integrated into the global economy as a supplier of raw materials rather than as an emerging industrial power.

In addition to this economic legacy, Ali's reforms reshaped Egypt's culture and society. They transformed the country's educational standards and built the foundations for a modern system of higher education. This new educational system produced a Western-oriented intelligentsia fully engaged with European intellectual life. They brought the ideas of the Enlightenment and nationalism into Egyptian public discourse, which included expectations for the rule of law, checks on executive power, and self-government. These ideas would take hold later in the nineteenth century and lead to calls from middle- and upper-class Egyptians for constraints on the power of the Khedive.

Ali's successors as Khedive (Abbas, Said, Ismail, and Tewfiq) continued the broad outlines of his approach to building Egypt. Ismail, in particular, invested heavily in irrigation and infrastructure. His biggest project was the Suez Canal, which opened in 1869. Through a series of poorly negotiated agreements with his French partners, Ismail allowed Egypt to assume almost all of the cost of construction. The Canal was built almost entirely by Egyptian laborers who worked under appalling conditions, often digging with their bare hands for little or no pay. Ismail borrowed heavily from European financial houses to pay for the Canal and his other projects. By 1875, he had accumulated debts of 100 million Egyptian pounds—roughly 10 times the country's annual tax revenue. The government was unable to generate enough cash to make the interest payments, let alone pay off the principal. In order to cope with this financial crisis, Ismail sold Egypt's shares in the Suez Canal to the British government in 1875. Britain gained control of 44 percent of the Suez Canal Company and later intervened militarily to protect its interests in the Canal.

The extent of Egypt's debts also led Britain and France to insist on a broader role in the day-to-day operations of the Egyptian government. In the 1870s, British and French officials assumed control of the ministries responsible for collecting taxes and managing the national budget. Europeans also expanded the use of a long-standing Ottoman institution, known as "the Capitulations," which exempted their nationals in Egypt from Egyptian laws. Under the Capitulations, a European citizen who committed a crime was tried according to the laws of his home country at his country's embassy in Cairo or its consulate in Alexandria, rather than in Egyptian courts. Europeans were generally treated leniently by their consulates and embassies. They could break the law or evade taxation with few repercussions, which sparked public anger over the wealth and privilege of the European minority. This anger would help fuel Egypt's nationalist movement in the latter part of the nineteenth century.

Ismail's financial difficulties had other important repercussions. Egypt's landowners worried that Ismail might increase taxes or, possibly, seize their property in order to pay the country's debts. This fear led to a growing demand to create institutions that could check the Khedive's power. Toward this end, Egypt created its first Parliament in 1866. The assembly was hardly a representative institution—only landowners could serve in the body or vote for its members. It also had no meaningful power to draft legislation. However, Parliament evolved into an important arena for debate among the landowning elite and became a forum for advocates of greater constraints on executive authority.

Toward the end of the nineteenth century, one of the tensions stemming from Muhammad Ali's military reforms erupted at the center of Egyptian politics. As mentioned earlier, Ali substantially expanded the Egyptian army and allowed native-born Egyptians to serve in the officer corps through the rank of captain. By the 1870s, four native-born Egyptians were also permitted to hold the rank of colonel. However, all other senior officers were Turkish or Circassian. As Egypt's financial problems deepened in the 1870s, its European financial advisors—who now controlled the country's budget—announced plans to shrink the Egyptian military in order to save money. The brunt of this cost-cutting plan would fall on the native-born Egyptians in the military, particularly Egyptian officers. The prospect of shrinking their numbers brought simmering anger among the Egyptian officers to a boil. One of the Egyptian colonels, Ahmad Urabi, called on Khedive Ismail to reject the austerity plan and dismiss the British and French officials who drafted it. To the surprise of many, he complied. Britain responded by removing Khedive Ismail (with the help of the Ottoman Sultan) and replacing him with his more pliable son, Tewfiq. Urabi was arrested, but was soon released when his troops stormed the prison where he was held. Urabi promptly declared himself the leader of the country. Tewfiq fled to Alexandria and called on the British to support him. The British asserted that the safety and property of foreigners were at risk and invaded in 1882, bombarding the port of Alexandria. They proclaimed that the intervention would be limited to removing Urabi and restoring Tewfiq to power. However, Egypt had assumed an important strategic role in the British Empire as a source of resources for the British economy and as a transit point (through the Suez Canal) to India and Asia. Britain's supposedly brief stay lasted 74 years, until 1956, although a countrywide uprising after World War I led Britain to formally declare Egypt independent in 1922.

What Was the Impact of the British Occupation on Egypt?

British policy in Egypt was dominated for 24 years by a single official, Evelyn Baring, the first Earl of Cromer. A diplomat, Lord Cromer (as he became known) was sent to Egypt as part of an international commission to manage repayment of the international debts incurred by Khedive Ismail and his successors after Egypt declared bankruptcy in 1876. Once Britain put down the Urabi revolt, Lord Cromer came to exercise all the authority of a colonial viceroy even though Britain did not formally declare Egypt a colony. Lord Cromer appointed British officials throughout the Egyptian government and made clear to Egyptian ministers that they must follow British instructions or resign. Cromer wanted Egypt to make two key contributions to the Empire: supply the long staple cotton needed for Britain's textile industry; and guarantee the security of transportation through the Suez Canal, which had become an essential conduit for maintaining Britain's military and economic power in Asia.

Cromer intensified the focus of the Egyptian economy on the export of raw materials, particularly cotton, by presiding over extensive improvements in Egypt's irrigation and transportation networks. He assigned little priority to industrial development and structured the tax system to discourage the growth of Egyptian manufacturing. From Britain's standpoint, stronger Egyptian industries would consume raw materials that would otherwise go to Britain. These local industries might also compete with British manufacturers. Cromer also frowned upon improving the Egyptian education system. In his view, a better-educated Egyptian population might demand greater rights and, possibly, independence—neither of which served British interests. He made little effort to develop Egypt's political institutions and asserted that Egyptians were not capable of governing themselves. Cromer's term as consul came to an end in 1907. His successors continued his economic and educational policies with little modification. They allowed the Egyptian Parliament to re-emerge, but granted it little meaningful authority. Parliament remained a forum for landowning elites to express their views on policy matters but had little relevance for ordinary Egyptians.

Public resentment of the British presence grew toward the end of Cromer's rule, particularly after a brutal crackdown in 1906 on a group of villagers accused of killing a British soldier in what became known as the Denshwai incident. Public anger rose further during World War I (1914–1918), when Britain stationed over 400,000 troops in Egypt. These troops consumed large amounts of food and other goods, which drove up prices for ordinary Egyptians. The British also seized farm animals for use in their campaign, which left many peasants with no means for plowing their land. In addition, the British cashiered thousands of Egyptian peasants to perform menial labor in support of British troops in Palestine. Even Egypt's landowners resented British policy, which required them to grow food for British troops rather than cotton for export.

As the war drew to a close, demands for an end to British rule were heard at every level of Egyptian society. Calls from international leaders for self-determination, particularly those by US president Woodrow Wilson, reinforced the determination of Egyptian nationalists. Wilson's "Fourteen Points" for organizing world affairs after World War I were translated into Arabic and distributed widely. They led many Egyptians to believe that their moment for independence had arrived.

What Were the Origins of Egyptian Nationalism?

A prominent historian of Egypt, Afaf Lutfi al-Sayyid Marsot, writes that Egypt's nationalist movement was made up of three groups: landowners who sought a constitutional regime to constrain the Khedive and limit British interference in the economy; intellectuals, many of whom had studied in Europe and were eager to apply European nationalist ideas to Egypt; and Egyptian military officers, who resented the presence of non-Egyptians (Turks and Circassians) in the most senior military posts and who feared that these senior officers served foreign rather than Egyptian interests.[1]

As mentioned earlier, Egyptian army officers took the lead by initiating the Urabi revolt in 1882. While Britain suppressed this call for greater independence, the demand resurfaced after World War I. A prominent Egyptian judge, Saad Zaghloul, led a group of Egyptians who met with the British High Commissioner and asked to send a delegation (a *Wafd*, in Arabic) to the Versailles peace conference to negotiate for Egyptian independence. The request was denied and Zaghloul was exiled to Malta. Zaghloul's exile triggered widespread public demonstrations in 1919 against the British presence. The British finally acquiesced and allowed Zaghloul and the Wafd to travel to Versailles, where the assembled leaders, including Woodrow Wilson, rejected their petition for independence. The rejection of the Wafd's petition deepened public anger and frustration and led to another round of demonstrations. Britain had neither the resources nor the will to suppress Egypt's nationalist movement. Instead, the British granted Egypt independence in 1922 but with sharp constraints. Britain gave itself the right to maintain troops in Egypt, to control the Suez Canal, to protect foreigners and minorities, and to determine Egyptian foreign policy. While these constraints on sovereignty clearly left the country short of full independence, Egypt was nonetheless recognized as a new nation and became a member of the League of Nations.

What Was Egypt's "Liberal Experiment" in the 1920s and 1930s?

Since the mid-nineteenth century, Egypt's Westernized elite had regularly called for strengthening the rule of law and constraining the power of the Khedive. With the advent of independence in 1922, this elite had an opportunity to reshape Egypt's government in a more liberal direction. The clearest example of their efforts was the Constitution of 1923, which established a two-chamber Parliament. The lower house (*Majlis al-Shaab*) was chosen through free elections in which all adult citizens were eligible to vote and run for office. In the upper house (*Majlis al-Shura*), the king appointed the president and two-fifths of its members. The remainder was chosen through free elections involving all adult citizens, but only large landowners were permitted to run for office. The king and the Parliament jointly exercised legislative power. The 1923 Constitution guaranteed freedom of expression and assembly and asserted the equality of all citizens before the law regardless of race, language, or religion.

Despite the potential of the 1923 Constitution, Egypt failed to establish a liberal democratic order. An open political system threatened both Britain and the king. Britain feared that democratic politics would strengthen anti-British sentiment, while King Fuad feared further constraints on his power. Free elections in January 1924 brought the Wafd Party under Saad Zaghloul to power. Britain found Zaghloul's nationalist policies unacceptable and pressured the king to replace him. The king complied and then, in 1930, abrogated the 1923 Constitution, replacing it with a new Constitution that broadened his powers. He then suspended this Constitution in 1934. When the Wafd finally returned to politics in 1935, it had tired of political isolation and adopted a less belligerent stand toward the British. The party negotiated an accord in 1936 that allowed Britain to keep troops in the Suez Canal region for another 20 years.

The Wafd compromised its nationalist principles even more dramatically a few years later. As World War II widened, the British were deeply concerned that Egypt's government was sympathetic to Germany. In February 1942, British forces surrounded the royal palace and forced the king to appoint a Wafdist government, which the British believed would be more consistently anti-German. The willingness of the Wafd to take power after what was, in essence, a British coup further discredited the party and the semi-democratic process that it helped to build. The party that had fought so ardently for the nationalist cause was now seen as cooperating fully with the occupying power. When the Wafd left office in 1944, its opponents launched a blistering campaign that accused the party of corruption, collusion with the British, and abuse of power. The Wafd retaliated with its own charges of corruption by the king and other members of the political elite. Whatever the degree of truth in these charges and countercharges, the mudslinging and political bickering thoroughly discredited the liberal experiment that had begun in the 1920s. When Gamal Abdel Nasser carried out a military coup in 1952 that removed the country's political leaders, virtually no one was willing to defend them. Nasser abrogated the Constitution in 1952.

Why Did a Women's Rights Movement Emerge in the Early Twentieth Century?

Egypt's liberal experiment included a movement for women's rights. A prominent lawyer, Qasim Amin, wrote *The Liberation of Women* in 1899, which argued that Egypt's weakness relative to Europe was due partially to its treatment of women. He called for ending the veiling of women and for expanding their educational opportunities. As the Egyptian nationalist movement gained momentum in the early twentieth century, women played an increasingly important role in politics and public debate. In the 1919 uprising against Britain, women participated in the demonstrations and issued a statement calling for independence and expanded women's rights. In the early 1920s, a prominent woman from an aristocratic family—Huda Shaarawi—founded the Egyptian feminist union and announced that she would no longer wear the veil. She argued that Egypt's struggle for independence and the rights of women were intertwined and that Egypt could not be truly independent until all of its citizens were equal.

What Was the Islamic Reformist Movement?

The sentiments and political developments that fueled Egyptian nationalism also sparked an Islamic reformist movement in the late nineteenth and early twentieth centuries. This movement emerged, as did the nationalist movement, from anger at the extent of British involvement in Egypt and, more generally, from an acute awareness of Egypt's weakness relative to Europe. For the nationalists, the solution to this problem lay in embracing European concepts of national independence and constitutionalism in order to achieve sovereignty and self-government. Most of the leaders of this movement were secular, and called for limiting religion's role in public life. For Islamic reformers, the solution lay in reinvigorating Islam. In their view, Egypt was weak and easily penetrated by Britain and others because the doctrine and institutions of Islam had been corrupted by centuries of inept leadership. The solution to this problem lay not in emulating European institutions and ideas, but in returning to the country's Islamic traditions and beliefs. By reviving and reinvigorating the Islamic faith, Egypt would achieve the unity and sense of purpose needed to restore its glory. Leading Islamic reformers such as Jamal al-Din al-Afghani, Muhammad Abdou, and Rashid Rida asserted that Islam should be rethought from its foundations. This process entailed returning to the core texts of the faith—the Quran and the Sunnah (the sayings and actions of the prophet)—and reinterpreting these texts to reflect modern conditions.

Islamic reformers were strong advocates of Egyptian independence, on the grounds that non-Muslim foreigners would never allow Egypt to achieve its true greatness as an Islamic nation. They supported educational reforms that included the study of science and technology. In their view, Islam was compatible with reason and science. A careful reinterpretation of the faith could integrate spirituality, reason, science, and technology into a cohesive worldview that could guide the lives of individual Muslims and the policies of the nation.

One of the most prominent reformers, Muhammad Abdou, became Mufti of Egypt in 1899. This post enabled him to issue authoritative legal opinions on many of the issues of the day. His rulings included allowing Muslims to wear European clothing, permitting banks to charge interest on loans, and broadening women's opportunities for education. Both al-Afghani and Abdou supported the establishment of a constitutional government that would clearly define the purposes of executive power and limit the ruler's authority. Abdou's student, Rashid Rida, shared the view that Islam needed fundamental reform in order to meet the demands of modern life. However, he differed from his predecessors in calling for the restoration of Islamic government in the form of a Caliphate. This government would be based on consultation between the Caliph and the members of the Islamic community, which would lead to laws that respected the public's preferences and served the public interest. However, Rida did not spell out how this process of consultation would occur.

What Are the Major Strands of Egyptian Identity?

Egypt's extraordinarily long history, combined with its location at the intersection of many empires and civilizations over the millennia, gives it an abundance of possible identities. At various moments over the past two centuries, Egyptian politicians and intellectuals emphasized different aspects of this historical experience in search of a distinctly Egyptian character and vision.

The Egyptian nationalists of the early twentieth century asserted that Egypt's distinct identity lay primarily in its rich pharaonic history. They argued that Egyptians had been a single nation for millennia and that the greatness of the pharaonic era showed the enormous potential of a unified Egyptian people. Pharaonic imagery, particularly the pyramids, became a central motif of nationalist newspapers and political pamphlets. When the hero of Egypt's independence struggle,

Saad Zaghloul, died in 1927, he was memorialized with a tomb modeled on a pharaonic temple. Early nationalists also asserted that Egyptian identity included a connection to Mediterranean civilizations. Egypt had been home to Greek, Roman, and Byzantine dynasties that were among the richest and most powerful of their times. These civilizations were part of the rich tapestry of Egyptian identity.

When Gamal Abdel Nasser became the leader of Egypt after the 1952 coup, he emphasized several other features of Egyptian identity. In his *Philosophy of the Revolution*, he wrote that Egypt stood at the intersection of three circles of civilization: Arab, Islamic, and African. In his view, Egypt incorporated each of these civilizations and combined them to produce a distinctly Egyptian ethos. As Nasser assumed a more prominent position in the Arab nationalist movement in the 1950s and 1960s, he particularly emphasized Egypt's Arab identity and the leadership role in the region that flowed from it.

Some secular reformers of the 1980s and 1990s emphasized the country's long-standing relationship with Europe and argued that Egypt was a natural bridge between Europe and the Arab and Islamic worlds. Toward this end, they called for strengthening the rule of law and for broadening democracy. They aimed to combine Western institutions of law and governance with Egyptian culture and traditions to produce a uniquely Egyptian form of participatory government. In contrast, one of the primary opposition movements of the twentieth century—the Muslim Brotherhood—emphasized Egypt's Islamic identity and its important contributions to Islamic civilization. The Brotherhood, discussed in Chapter 6, asserted that Egypt's natural role lies in leading its fellow Muslim states.

Debates over Egyptian identity have been integrated into competitions for political power for decades, with politicians drawing on the stream of identity that best legitimizes their political aspirations. The struggle over Egyptian identity is thus closely tied to competing political visions for the country.

Suggested Readings

For a general history of Egypt from the pharaohs to the present, Robert Tignor's *Egypt: A Short History* (Princeton, 2010) provides a thorough and readable overview. For a discussion that focuses on modern Egypt (1805 to the present), see Afaf Lutfi al-Sayyid Marsot, *A Short History of Modern Egypt* (Cambridge, 1985). For a more detailed account of this period, see P. J. Vatikiotis, *The History of Modern Egypt: From Muhammad Ali to Mubarak* (Johns Hopkins, 1991). There are several fine works on Muhammad Ali and his era. One of the best is Khaled Fahmy, *All the Pasha's Men: Mehmed Ali, His Army, and the Making of Modern Egypt* (Cambridge, 1997). For a wonderful discussion of the cultural and social conditions at the end of the nineteenth century that led to the rise of Egyptian nationalism, read Juan Ricardo Cole, *Colonialism and Revolution in the Middle East: Social and Cultural Origins of Egypt's 'Urabi Movement* (Princeton, 1993). For further analysis of Egyptian nationalism, see Israel Gershoni and James P. Jankowski, *Redefining the Egyptian Nation, 1930–1945* (Cambridge, 1995).
Britain's presence in Egypt has fascinated scholars and chroniclers of all types. For an excellent study of Britain's impact, see Robert L. Tignor, *Modernization and British Colonial Rule in Egypt, 1882–1914* (Princeton, 1966). For a thoughtful discussion of Lord Cromer, the architect of most of Britain's policies in Egypt, see Roger Owen, *Lord Cromer: Victorian Imperialist, Edwardian Proconsul* (Oxford, 2004). After Britain granted Egypt independence in 1922, the country embarked on an ill-fated attempt to establish a liberal constitutional government. Afaf Lutfi al-Sayyid Marsot provides a careful and thoughtful assessment of this effort in *Egypt's Liberal Experiment, 1922–1936* (University of California Press, 1977). Beth Baron examines the emergence of Egypt's feminist movement in *The Women's Awakening in Egypt—Culture, Society, and Press* (Yale, 1994). The Islamic reform movement has been analyzed by a wide range of historians, political scientists, and scholars of religion. One of the finest works on this topic is Albert Hourani, *Arabic Thought in the Liberal Age, 1798–1939* (Cambridge, 1983).

3

BUILDING A NEW REGIME

NASSER, SADAT, AND MUBARAK

*What Caused the Military Coup in 1952? What Were
Its Goals?*

The political order created after Egypt's independence in 1922 was a disappointment to many Egyptians. The struggle for power among the Wafd Party, other political parties, the king, and the British produced a chaotic and dysfunctional political system in which factionalism and violence increasingly marred political life. The landowning elites that dominated Parliament were unable to address the country's growing economic challenges and unwilling to deal with the enormous disparity in income between a very wealthy elite and a largely impoverished population. By some estimates, at the time of the 1952 coup, 12,000 landowners controlled a third of the country's arable land while 11 million peasants went landless.[1]

The government was also unable to limit the continued British presence in the country. The Anglo-Egyptian treaty of 1936 stated that Britain could deploy no more than 10,000 troops to protect the Suez Canal. After World War II, this figure reached over 80,000 as the defense of the Canal became central to British and American strategy during the Cold War. Many members of Egypt's military resented the government's failure to defend the country's sovereignty in the face of a de facto occupation of the Canal zone. Their anger grew further when the Egyptian army performed poorly during the 1948 war that brought Israel into existence. Many officers attributed the defeat to corrupt politicians who sent defective weapons and spoiled food to Egypt's front line troops. Among the disillusioned soldiers was a young officer, Gamal Abdel Nasser, who had been wounded while fighting in the Negev desert.

Nasser began to organize like-minded mid-level officers (the "Free Officers") who shared his disdain for the current political order and who felt that the military was the only institution that could deliver Egypt from its weakness and malaise. They seized power on July 23, 1952. They forced King Farouq to abdicate and appointed a prominent general, Muhammad Naguib, to serve as president. However, tensions between Naguib and Nasser intensified and Naguib was forced out in 1954. Nasser became prime minister and then, in 1956, president.

The new regime moved quickly to transform the country. The cornerstone of this effort was land reform, in which the government seized the largest estates and distributed them to peasants. After several amendments, the land reform law placed an upper limit of roughly 50 acres on individual land ownership—a dramatic change from the pre-1952 situation, when some families owned many thousands of acres. The royal family alone reputedly held 180,000 acres at the time of the coup.

As Nasser consolidated power in the 1950s and early 1960s, the regime became tightly centralized. The government dismantled Egypt's semi-competitive political system and banned opposition parties, on the grounds that they aggravated divisions in society. Nasser established instead a single ruling party, the Arab Socialist Union (ASU). He also replaced independent associations for workers and professionals with state-controlled unions and professional syndicates. The state took control of radio, television, and newspapers. In addition, the regime nationalized virtually all of the country's industries and established large state-owned firms that dominated every sector of the economy.

At the heart of this order was a new ruling bargain. The state would provide for the basic needs of citizens through an extensive array of subsidies on goods and services. In exchange, citizens would stay out of politics and follow the lead of the president and the ruling party. Borrowing from the examples of the Soviet Union and Central Europe, this new political order reflected the principle that the state embodied the will of the people and would mobilize and deploy the country's resources on the nation's behalf. Nasser and his followers believed that this centralized and technocratic style of governance would produce more rapid growth than a market economy, which, in their view, was easily manipulated by domestic and international businessmen. In reality, however, as in the former Soviet Union, the state apparatus simply could not adequately administer a complex national economy. Egypt's centrally managed economy led to inefficiencies in pricing and production, rising levels of domestic debt, and sharp declines in private investment.

What Were the Key Institutions of Nasser's Regime?

Three institutions were particularly important for maintaining and extending the state's control over society: the state-owned sector, the subsidy system, and the bureaucracy.

State-owned sector: With the sweeping nationalization of private firms in the early 1960s, the regime brought virtually all of the country's productive enterprises under state control. The state-owned sector became the driving force of the economy. It served three fundamental purposes. First, it enabled the state to control the commanding heights of the economy and direct investment toward sectors prioritized by the government, particularly heavy industry and consumer goods. Second, state-owned industries sold these goods to citizens at affordable, state-controlled prices. Although the quality of these goods was often poor, they nonetheless enabled many Egyptians to enjoy a higher standard of living. Finally, the state-owned sector provided employment for many thousands of Egyptians. The expansion of the state-owned sector under Nasser is striking. By 1965, investment in this sector made up 98 percent of gross domestic fixed investment. This figure remained above 75 percent well into the 1980s. The percentage of GDP originating in the state-owned sector increased from roughly 13 percent in 1952 to about 40 percent by 1969, while employment in this sector rose from 400,000 in 1960 to 965,000 in 1970.[2]

Subsidies: One of the foundations of the Free Officers' revolution was their pledge to improve social justice and reduce inequality. At the heart of this effort was an extensive system of subsidies designed to ensure that every Egyptian could afford basic goods and services. The state sought to provide food, electricity, gasoline, public transportation, education, medical care, and other services for free or at heavily subsidized prices. However, implementation of the subsidies was often flawed. They were applied more effectively in the cities than in the countryside, which led to increased rural-urban migration. In addition, subsidies were not adequately targeted toward the neediest citizens. In some cases, wealthy citizens used more of these goods and services than the poor.

As international prices for key commodities such as wheat rose, subsidies consumed an ever-greater portion of the government budget. In 1975, subsidies cost the government 622 million LE. By 1990, they cost 4.6 billion LE. Over the period 1965 to 1990, subsidies absorbed 18 percent of total government expenditure. In some years, the figure could be much higher. For example, from 1975 to 1981, subsidies consumed 22 percent of total government expenditure.[3]

Bureaucracy: The state-led development strategy embraced by Nasser stressed that the state embodied the aspirations of the people. The knowledge and expertise of government officials, combined with their commitment to the public good, was supposed to enable public agencies to make sound choices that guided national development. In Nasser's Egypt, the state would not only make all key decisions for the country: it would also implement these decisions and monitor their effectiveness. The regime accordingly built a vast bureaucracy to carry out these many complex tasks. The bureaucracy also became a key source of employment. Indeed, as its efficiency in performing its core tasks steadily declined, the bureaucracy's primary contribution lay in buttressing social and political stability by providing large numbers of poorly paid but secure jobs. At the time of the coup in 1952, about 350,000 persons were employed in the civilian public bureaucracy. By 1970, the figure was 1.2 million. This represented a growth rate of 7.2 percent per year, well in excess of the 2.2 percent annual growth rate in the national workforce. The number of government ministries doubled from 15 to 30 between 1952 and 1970.[4]

These three institutions were essential to the Nasser regime. They allowed the government to expand its influence over society by offering employment and consumer goods while also setting wages and prices. The state's dominance of the economy also gave it the resources needed to develop a large and intrusive intelligence service that monitored individuals and organizations. A small agency focused on gathering intelligence for the police force was expanded into the General Directorate of State Security Investigations (SSI). Individuals belonging to suspected opposition groups—including socialists, communists, "feudalists," and Islamists—were particularly targeted. The SSI was also in charge of vetting candidates for mid-level and senior positions throughout the state and society, including leaders of professional associations, universities, and state-owned enterprises. In addition, Nasser established the Central Security Forces (*al-Amn al-Markazi*) as the front-line troops for controlling protests and riots, which enabled him to avoid relying entirely on the military or the regular police for domestic security.

How Did Nasser Alter Egypt's Economy?

Nasser believed that Egypt's weakness was tied to the structure of its economy. He argued that the colonial powers had purposely kept Egypt under-industrialized in order to focus the country's economic activity on providing cotton, sugar cane, and other raw materials. Under this system, Egypt exported its raw materials at low prices set by the colonial nations and then spent its precious foreign exchange to import the finished products needed to meet the needs of its people. Nasser sought to transform this economic structure by making Egypt self-sufficient. Like other postcolonial leaders after World War II, he adopted a policy of Import Substitution Industrialization (ISI), under which Egypt would build the industrial capacity to meet most of its needs. This strategy involved constructing a sprawling state-owned industrial sector that produced everything from television sets to automobiles. It also entailed adopting high tariff barriers against the import of industrial goods, in order to protect Egypt's infant industries. For example, foreign automobiles faced a 1000 percent tariff before they could be sold in Egypt.

At its height, this approach led to the government directing almost every aspect of the country's industrial development. Government officials decided which industries and sectors would receive investment, the wages they would pay, the prices for their goods, and where their goods would be sold. As with other centrally planned economies, however, the state apparatus simply could not accurately collect and analyze enough information to allocate resources efficiently. This led to the emergence of informal markets and illicit black markets that helped to meet the public's demand for goods and services.

Why Did Nasser Build the Aswan High Dam?
What Were the Effects of the Dam?

In order to industrialize rapidly, Egypt needed an ample supply of electricity to power its factories. Toward this end, Nasser proposed building a new dam on the Nile at Aswan that would generate hydroelectric power and create a massive reservoir to ensure a reliable supply of water even in times of drought. At the time, the dam was the largest ever attempted anywhere in the world.

The idea of building dams along the Nile for flood control and drought protection was not new. The British had proposed several dams along the tributaries of the Nile, primarily the White Nile and the Blue Nile further upstream, and had already constructed a smaller dam at Aswan. Nasser's proposal to site the dam near Aswan had the obvious advantage of giving Egypt control over the Nile's flow within its territory. However, the dam was controversial among international water planners, who observed that its reservoir would evaporate rapidly in Egypt's heat and lead to substantial water loss compared to building dams further upstream in the highlands of Ethiopia or Kenya.

Nasser needed funding and technical assistance for such a massive project. He sought both from the World Bank and the United States, but the United States was wary of Nasser's charismatic appeal in the Arab world and his embrace of pan-Arab nationalism. His call to unite the Arab countries into an anti-colonial alliance of new republics threatened monarchies in Jordan, Saudi Arabia, Iran, and Kuwait that were allies of the United States and Britain. The United States dragged its feet during the negotiations as it sought ways to work with Nasser and blunt the popularity of his rhetoric and agenda.

In frustration, Nasser turned to the USSR and the Eastern bloc countries under its control. In 1955, Egypt announced that it would acquire weapons from Czechoslovakia. Nasser also asserted that Egypt would remain neutral in the Cold War

("non-aligned") and, thus, it would engage in economic and
military transactions with both the Soviet Union and the West.
However, American officials, particularly the US secretary of
state John Foster Dulles, believed the arms deal showed that
Egypt had moved decisively into the communist orbit. Their
concerns deepened when Nasser extended diplomatic rec-
ognition to the People's Republic of China in May 1956. The
United States responded by terminating negotiations over
American and World Bank assistance for constructing the new
Aswan dam.

Nasser reacted with an even more provocative step: he
nationalized the British-controlled Suez Canal in July 1956.
The Egyptian government compensated the shareholders
of the Canal based on the value of their shares at the time of
the nationalization and then began operating the Suez Canal
Authority as a state-owned enterprise. Nasser hoped that the
revenue generated by collecting tolls on ships passing through
the Canal would supply enough capital to construct the Aswan
dam. Britain did not take the nationalization sitting down and
invaded Egypt in 1956 alongside France and Israel with the
goal of retaking the Canal. However, as explained below, the
invasion failed and Egypt retained control of the Canal.

Egypt ultimately relied heavily on Soviet financial and
technical support to complete the Dam, which became fully
operational in 1970. It produced about 50 percent of the
country's electricity in the 1970s. The Dam's reservoir, Lake
Nasser, allows for a managed flow of water throughout the
year and stores enough water to sustain Egypt even when severe droughts upstream reduced the river's flow. The result
has been a sharp increase in agricultural output. However, the
Dam also has serious negative environmental effects. It blocks
the flow of rich silt from the upper reaches of the Nile, which
had been an essential source of nutrients to restore the soil.
Instead, Egyptian farmers must use large quantities of expensive fertilizers to sustain the soil's productivity. The lack of silt
also contributes to the Nile Delta slowly subsiding into the sea,

as soil that is eroded by the river's flow and the Mediterranean Sea is no longer replaced by silt from upstream.

How Central Was the Military to Nasser's Regime?

At the heart of the 1952 coup was the Free Officers' belief that only the military could rescue the country from its sorry condition. In their view, Egypt's fitful attempt at democracy in the period between the two world wars had led to a small and well-connected elite dominating the country. Political parties were little more than the playthings of self-interested elites, and Parliament was a bazaar where selfish politicians maneuvered for individual gain. In contrast, Nasser and the Free Officers believed that the military could speak for the people and advance their interests. Nasser often reminded Egyptians that military officers came from the same humble backgrounds as most Egyptians and understood their concerns. Furthermore, their military training provided them with the skills and the discipline needed to lead the country to greatness.

Nasser put this view into action almost immediately. As he consolidated power and extended his influence over politics and the economy, he appointed military officers to almost all of the senior positions of leadership. In addition to the country's defenses, they led the growing domestic security and intelligence agencies and the ministries responsible for censorship and propaganda. They controlled the newly established ruling party and ran the country's growing bureaucracy as well as the new state-owned enterprises that were the cornerstone of Nasser's economic strategy.

However, not all of Egypt's officers shared Nasser's vision. In the months following the coup, parts of the military resisted his efforts to centralize power and favored a more democratic order. Nasser acted decisively against these challengers in 1952 and 1954, but remained uncertain whether he enjoyed broad support among officers and the rank and file. He dealt with this uncertainty by appointing his closest friend, Abdel Hakim

Amer, as Minister of Defense. However, Amer built his own network of support within the officer corps that was more loyal to him than to Nasser. To complicate matters further, Amer was not a skilled general. He bore much of the responsibility for the poor performance of the Egyptian military during the 1956 war against Britain, France, and Israel. However, the breadth of his support within the officer corps prevented Nasser from removing him. Nasser dealt with the military's growing power and autonomy by building institutions that could counterbalance it—particularly, a larger domestic security apparatus and a larger ruling party, the ASU, which could mobilize the public on his behalf.

Nasser's relationship with the military underwent a dramatic change after the country's humiliating defeat in the 1967 war with Israel, which will be discussed in greater detail below. The scope of this defeat provided the grounds for Nasser to confront Amer and the rest of the military leadership. Senior military leaders were removed and prosecuted in public trials broadcast on national television. More than 1,000 officers were dismissed. Amer committed suicide. Nasser then appointed a new group of leaders to restore his power over the armed forces. He also expanded his control over the defense budget, arms procurement, and military appointments. The heads of each branch of the armed services now reported directly to him, rather than to the Minister of Defense. He also reduced the extent of the military's involvement in politics and the economy. Military appointees who directed state-owned firms were either demoted or replaced. The number of military officers in the cabinet declined sharply. Nasser's effort to strengthen his hold on the armed forces was still unfolding when he died in September 1970.

What Was Arab Nationalism?

The idea of a shared Arab identity, grounded in a common language and history, has its roots in the late nineteenth century. It emerged partly as a result of Arab intellectuals drawing from the example of European nationalists, particularly in Germany and France, who had built strong and prosperous nation-states based upon shared linguistic and cultural identities. It was also partly a product of structural changes in the Ottoman Empire, where the Sultan began favoring officials of Turkish descent over non-Turks in appointments to senior positions. As prominent Arabs were excluded from positions of power in Istanbul, some began to build greater autonomy and power in the Arab provinces that they managed. After the collapse of the Ottoman Empire in 1917, Arabs who had previously been part of provinces within the Empire began to organize as members of new states such as Syria, Jordan, and Iraq. Their efforts were facilitated by the new leader of Turkey, Mustapha Kemal Ataturk. Ataturk renounced Turkey's claim to Ottoman Arab lands and abolished the Caliphate, which had served as one of the central institutions of Islamic political and legal authority. With the institutions of Islamic identity in disarray, some intellectuals and political leaders called for basing the new states on a common Arab identity that embraced Muslims and Christians equally.

In Egypt, the idea of pan-Arab nationalism coexisted un-easily with the distinctive Egyptian identity emphasized by Egyptian nationalists such as Saad Zaghloul and his supporters. While these thinkers acknowledged an Arab di-mension to Egypt's identity, it was subordinate to the identity that flowed from the achievements of pharaonic history and civilization. Nasser retained this emphasis on the uniqueness and glory of Egypt. However, he also took up the mantle of Arab nationalism, particularly after his dramatic success in nationalizing the Suez Canal in 1956. This nationalization set off a brief war involving Britain, France, and Israel that aimed to regain the Canal for Britain and weaken Nasser. Due largely to American intercession, this effort failed and Nasser emerged from the 1956 war victorious. This success enabled Nasser to present himself as the only leader in the region who had confronted and defeated the imperial powers of Britain, France, and Israel.

With this victory in hand, Nasser argued that Egypt was the natural leader of the Arab world based on several considerations: many great Arab civilizations had been centered in Egypt, such as the Mamluk Empire; the country had the largest population and the largest economy in the Arab world; it played a uniquely influential role in Arab culture through literature, poetry, film, and music; and the country's large army enabled it to lead Arab resistance to the colonial powers. The 1956 Constitution proclaimed that Egypt was an Arab country and part of the Arab nation. Nasser presented himself as the representative of the Arabs to the world in settings such as the Non-Aligned Movement, which Nasser founded with Sukarno of Indonesia, Jawaharlal Nehru of India, Kwame Nkrumah of Ghana, and Josef Tito of Yugoslavia in 1961.

Nasser's view of Egypt as the leader of the Arab world led him to costly interventions in several disputes. He sent 70,000 troops to fight in a civil war in Yemen and sent money and weapons to Algerians fighting for independence from France. He also made the surprising decision to unify Egypt and Syria into a single country, the United Arab Republic (UAR), in 1958. He took this step at the request of Syrian leaders who believed it would bring stability to Syria. However, Nasser's conviction that Egyptians were the natural leaders of this new country was not shared by his Syrian counterparts, who resented Egypt's dominant role in the new state. These tensions came to a head in 1961, when a military coup in Damascus brought the UAR to an end.

Egyptian leaders continue to view their country as the natural leader of the Arab world. However, the rise of powerful oil-based monarchies in the Gulf in the 1970s eroded Egypt's preeminence. These monarchies enjoyed an enormous windfall of cash after the 1973 oil embargo that dramatically increased their regional power. Egypt's stature was further reduced by the country's 1979 peace treaty with Israel, which faced sharp criticism in the Arab world and led most Arab states to ostra-cize Egypt. President Mubarak gradually reversed this isola-tion in the 1980s and 1990s, but persistent economic weakness has limited Egypt's capacity to influence regional affairs.

What Impact Did the 1967 Arab-Israeli War Have on Nasserism?

Prior to the war, Nasser told the Egyptian people time and again that his government had rebuilt the military and that it could face any challenge. In his view, the most immediate challenge was Israel. He asserted repeatedly that his newly strengthened military could defeat Israel at any time and would do so in the near future.

Israel's military leaders took this threat seriously. In re-sponse to Egypt blockading the Gulf of Aqaba in May 1967 and withdrawing UN peacekeeping forces in Sinai, they destroyed Egypt's air force on June 6, 1967 and moved Israeli troops into Sinai. Jordan and Syria promptly entered the war on Egypt's side. Within six days, however, Israel secured a comprehen-sive victory that decimated the Egyptian military and led to Israeli troops occupying all of Sinai as well as the Gaza Strip. Israel also occupied the West Bank and East Jerusalem, which had been under Jordanian control, and the Golan Heights, which was Syrian territory. In the wake of this devastating defeat, Nasser announced his resignation. However, huge demonstrations—some organized by government agencies—persuaded him to reconsider. He remained in office until his death in 1970.

The psychological effect of the 1967 defeat on Egyptians is difficult to overstate. Nasser had claimed for years that his rev-olution had created a new Egypt with unrivaled economic, po-litical, and military power. Yet, when the clash with its greatest adversary finally occurred, Egypt was soundly defeated. As noted earlier, the scope of the defeat provided an opportu-nity to restructure the military and, particularly, to expand Nasser's direct control over military affairs. It also enabled him to reduce the military's role in domestic politics and security, on the grounds that it should focus all of its resources on preparing for the next war with Israel.

The 1967 war also had significant repercussions in the domestic political arena. Nasser had suppressed domestic critics partly on the grounds that national unity must be maintained while the country prepared to confront Israel. In response to the defeat, he made a small effort to open the political system and allowed limited press freedom. Some professional associations, such as the Bar Association, took advantage of this opening to become vocal advocates for greater civil and political rights. However, the regime's repressive capabilities remained in place. Large demonstrations organized by students and workers in February and November 1968 were put down with brutal efficiency.

Finally, Egypt's defeat also pushed Nasser into closer cooperation with the Soviet Union. Because the United States had supplied Israel with weapons prior to the war, Nasser turned more decisively toward the Soviet Union. The Soviets obliged by replenishing Egypt's weapons stockpiles and by providing pilots, instructors, and technicians to train Egypt's soldiers and operate its air defenses. By 1972, over 20,000 Soviet advisors were deployed in Egypt.

How Did Egyptian Authoritarianism Change under Sadat?

Nasser died of a heart attack in September 1970 and was succeeded by his vice president, Anwar Sadat. Sadat was not a major figure in Nasser's regime. Indeed, some observers argued that Nasser appointed him vice president precisely because he was politically weak and therefore posed little threat. This perceived weakness led to an early challenge to his power from adversaries in the security apparatus and the military. Sadat confronted them decisively in 1971 and imprisoned many of them. He further believed that the Soviet Union had conspired with his opponents and, as a consequence, expelled the 20,000 Soviet advisors in 1972. This step was also part of a broader strategy to re-orient Egypt toward the United States. Sadat believed that the United States could pressure Israel to return the Sinai to Egypt and provide much-needed economic assistance.

As Sadat consolidated power, he constrained and weakened institutions that he considered threatening while bolstering those that he could control. Toward this end, he further limited the military's involvement in domestic security by expanding the role of the Ministry of Interior. He even empowered the security services to vet candidates for military appointments.

Sadat also adopted a different strategy for preserving his regime. Nasser imposed very tight internal controls and prevented any organized opposition to the state. Sadat, in contrast, calculated that a small political opening could enhance his regime's stability by allowing public anger to be expressed through peaceful means, rather than violent confrontation. In addition, more open political debate and a freer press would enable him to easily identify his opponents and direct his repressive apparatus accordingly.

Sadat was not a democrat, as he was not willing to share power with popularly elected parties or politicians. However, his regime was less repressive than Nasser's. He granted amnesty to thousands of political prisoners who had fallen afoul of Nasser. He reined in some of the most brutal and arbitrary institutions of the Nasser era, including those that had nationalized private property in a sweeping and sometimes illegal manner. In the mid-1970s, he allowed the Muslim Brotherhood—which had been viciously suppressed under Nasser—to re-emerge and organize on university campuses as a counterbalance to leftist student organizations. He also allowed the three main ideological currents within the ruling ASU to form their own political parties and then disbanded the ASU in 1978. The new parties represented the left, the center, and the right, and competed in the 1979 parliamentary elections. Nonetheless, Sadat remained in control of the political arena by ensuring the victory of his new governing party, the National Democratic Party (NDP). In the mid-1970s, freedom of the press also improved, until public anger over economic hardships and Sadat's controversial peace overtures to Israel in 1977 and 1978 led to a renewed crackdown.

Egypt's peace treaty with Israel in 1979 produced another wave of public criticism, driven largely by accusations that Sadat had abandoned the Palestinian cause and weakened Arab unity. Sadat responded by restoring the grip of authoritarian institutions. Restrictions on the press were intensified and regime opponents were increasingly persecuted. Sadat became particularly concerned about growing criticism from Islamists. The Islamic revolution in Iran in 1979, which led to the ouster of Sadat's friend the Shah, made a strong impression on him. He steadily tightened the screws on Islamic organizations and activists. This crackdown reached its height one month before his death, when he arrested thousands of Islamic activists along with other activists of every political stripe. An army lieutenant tied to a radical Islamic group (Egyptian Islamic Jihad) assassinated Sadat on October 6, 1981.

How Did Sadat Change Egypt's Economy?

The state-centered economic system created by Nasser contained several contradictions. The most basic tension lay in the regime's effort to create a comprehensive welfare state that provided decent jobs and extensive subsidies while, simultaneously, trying to achieve rapid economic growth. The state simply could not raise enough money to achieve both goals. Nasser chose to sustain the key features of the welfare state, but doing so drained capital that was essential for investment and economic development. At the same time, the country's population increased steadily by about 2.8 percent per year. More Egyptians meant more demand for the subsidized goods and services provided by the regime, which it could ill-afford.

As the population expanded and economic growth remained modest at best, the viability of the Nasserist system came into question. Its underlying weaknesses were made even more apparent after the 1967 war and the ensuing reconstruction of the military, which diverted large amounts of capital from productive economic investment. Furthermore, the country's foreign policy placed it at odds with the West and reduced its access to concessionary loans as well as modern technology.

Anwar Sadat inherited these problems when he came to power in 1970. They were aggravated by the expense of another war with Israel in 1973 and a sharp increase in the cost of imported food in 1974. However, in Sadat's view, the country's economic challenges were not structural. He believed the country merely faced a short-term fiscal shortfall that could be solved by attracting capital from the wealthy countries of the Persian Gulf and the West. In an effort to tap these resources, Sadat issued the October White Paper in 1974. The paper announced a series of reforms—the *infitah* (opening)—designed to make Egypt more attractive to foreign investment, particularly from the oil-exporting states of the Persian Gulf. These reforms allowed foreign investment in any economic sector and permitted foreign investors to own majority positions in firms. New projects were entitled to tax exemptions and duty-free import of equipment and raw materials. Several free zones were established where new businesses were not subject to Egyptian tax. Arab investors from the Persian Gulf were given additional advantages, such as the right to own urban real estate.

In the decade following the *infitah*, the Egyptian economy performed surprisingly well. GDP growth averaged 9 percent per year in real terms while real per capita income increased roughly 6 percent per year. The investment rate doubled from 13.7 percent of GDP in 1973 to 28.7 percent in 1985. However, most economists do not attribute this performance to economic changes brought about by the *infitah*. Rather, the country enjoyed a fortuitous inflow of resources from several sources. Oil production increased dramatically after the end of the 1973 war as negotiations with Israel allowed Egypt to regain control over oil fields in the Sinai Peninsula and the Gulf of Suez. The end of the 1973 war also allowed Egypt to reopen the Suez Canal in 1975 and reap an increase in earnings from Canal tolls. Rapid economic growth in the Gulf States following a sharp rise in oil prices in 1973 created an enormous demand for Egyptian expatriate workers, who sent their salaries home and provided yet another source of foreign exchange. Tourism receipts also rose, as did foreign economic and military aid.

This influx of funds alleviated the economic crisis that Sadat inherited and eliminated the pressure for structural reform. Indeed, each of the long-standing pillars of the regime—the state-owned sector, subsidies, and the bureaucracy—grew during the Sadat years. The percentage of GDP originating from state-owned firms rose from 40 percent in 1969 to 50 percent in 1981. The cost of subsidies rose from less than 2 percent of GDP in 1971 to 13 percent in 1980. The size of the bureaucracy grew from 1.2 million employees in 1970 to 1.9 million in 1978. The structural challenges to Egypt's economy remained and would come to haunt Sadat's successor, Hosni Mubarak.[5]

While the private sector expanded under Sadat, it was led by cautious businessmen whose prosperity relied on their close relationships with the state. A firm's success hinged on gaining the cooperation of state officials who controlled permits, contracts, and capital. Egypt's resurgent capitalism was dominated by a handful of large family-owned companies whose patriarchs had been especially successful at cultivating ties to the state. The Osman family, for example, became a major force in the construction sector. The Mansour family developed a vast retailing empire that includes the Egyptian franchises for McDonalds and Caterpillar as well as one of the largest real estate development companies in the country.

How Did Egypt's Political System Change under Mubarak?

Sadat was assassinated in October 1981. He was succeeded by his vice president, Hosni Mubarak, who initially signaled that his regime would be less repressive than Sadat's. He released many of the political activists whom Sadat had rounded up in the closing months of his rule. Like Sadat in the mid-1970s, Mubarak calculated that some political freedom was useful for allowing his critics to vent their anger and for identifying his opponents. He allowed opposition parties to criticize the government, although he did not permit them the resources and freedoms to develop strong ties with citizens at the local level. He allowed professional associations to criticize the regime, as well. This was particularly the case for the Bar Association, which became a vocal opponent of continued limits on civil and political rights. At times, he allowed the opposition press to investigate and criticize the government with striking boldness, although these periods of free expression were often followed by bouts of repression. Similarly, professional associations had their wings clipped by changes in legislation that limited their ability to express dissent.

Mubarak also issued legislation that enhanced the autonomy of the judiciary, partly in the hope that stronger judicial institutions would help to attract private investment. However, some judges used this newly found autonomy to issue rulings that constrained the executive in areas such as police abuse and the rigging of elections. The professional association for judges (the Judges Club) became a vocal advocate for improvements in the rule of law. Toward the end of his administration, Mubarak reined in the judges by appointing his supporters to senior posts and by threatening to slash the budget of the Judges Club.

Mubarak also adopted and expanded Sadat's strategy of allowing multiparty elections for both houses of Parliament. He permitted six elections for Parliament during his 29 years in office. However, as in Sadat's time, these elections were carefully managed to ensure the victory of the ruling NDP. Opposition groups, including the Muslim Brotherhood, were sometimes allowed to win a handful of seats but the NDP remained the dominant force. Parliament was less a deliberative body than a patronage machine that enabled supporters of Mubarak to gain greater access to state resources.

The political system remained dominated by the executive branch, which had the authority to initiate laws that Parliament invariably adopted. The executive also had the power to implement laws selectively. The government sometimes disregarded the legal code altogether by invoking the country's emergency law, which remained in force throughout Mubarak's time in power. Presidential elections remained a very limited affair. The president was nominated by Parliament, which Mubarak controlled, and then the citizenry voted up or down in a national referendum that was often manipulated to produce "yes" votes of 90 percent or higher. In 2005, Mubarak relented to American pressure and allowed an election for the presidency. However, it was a heavily managed contest that led to Mubarak winning with 88 percent of the vote. His opponent, a lawyer named Ayman Nour, faced constant harassment by state media and security institutions during the election and was imprisoned soon after the results were announced.

What Economic Reforms Did Mubarak Adopt?

Mubarak inherited the same structural economic problems that Sadat faced. In essence, Nasser had created a social contract with the population that promised every citizen a large array of subsidies in exchange for their political support. Limited economic growth, coupled with high population growth, made this contract difficult to sustain under Sadat. It became impossible under Mubarak.

A drop in global oil prices that began in 1983 created particularly serious challenges. Egypt has never been a major oil exporter, but its steady production of a modest quantity of oil provided an important source of foreign exchange used to import food, spare parts, and finished goods. Oil revenues fell by 66 percent between 1983 and 1987, which reduced Egypt's import capacity by 12 percent. Falling oil prices also led to a recession in the Persian Gulf, which reduced opportunities for overseas employment for Egyptians. The number of Egyptians working in Arab Gulf countries fell from roughly 3 million in the early 1980s to less than 1 million in 1987. Many expatriate Egyptians returned home from the Gulf and joined the ranks of the unemployed. Tourism revenue—the country's third largest source of foreign exchange—was also down due to a series of terrorist incidents in Egypt and elsewhere in the region. The government attempted to cope with this financial crisis through a dramatic increase in foreign borrowing. Interest payments on external debt tripled between 1982 and 1987. If calculated using the free market rate, Egypt's debts in 1987 were equivalent to 184 percent of GDP, which made Egypt one of the most heavily indebted countries in the world. Egypt was caught in a classic debt trap, taking on new debt to acquire the funds needed to service existing debts. By 1987, new loans were not sufficient to cover the payments coming due.[6]

This precarious economic situation tipped into crisis in 1990. The economy had grown very little in the previous two years; unemployment was estimated at 20 percent, inflation was 20 percent annually, and external debt had continued to grow. GDP per capita had fallen from US$ 750 in 1985/1986 to US$ 640 in 1989/1990.

The Gulf War, which began with Iraq's invasion of Kuwait in August 1990, only worsened this situation. Over 400,000 Egyptian workers were forced to leave jobs in Iraq and Kuwait, dramatically reducing foreign remittances and aggravating unemployment in Egypt. Tourism receipts fell sharply as travelers avoided the Middle East, and Suez Canal revenues declined as shipping and trade shrank.

However, Egypt's willingness to assume a leadership role in opposing the Iraqi invasion produced a bonanza of economic rewards. Mubarak condemned Saddam Hussein's invasion and sent over 30,000 Egyptian troops to help liberate Kuwait. In return, roughly 50 percent of its foreign debt was forgiven in the years following the war, primarily by the Arab Persian Gulf States, the United States, and Europe. At the same time, the Gulf, Europe, the United States, Japan, South Korea, the World Bank, and the IMF provided large increases in economic aid. The country received US$7 billion in emergency assistance during the Gulf war, in order to ease the economic strains of the conflict. It received another US$8 billion after the war.

Much of this debt forgiveness and aid was conditioned on significant economic reforms. Private creditors, in particular, insisted that Egypt comply with the terms of an International Monetary Fund (IMF) restructuring program. Egypt entered into intensive negotiations with the IMF, and reached an agreement in May 1991. This agreement aimed to transform Egypt into a competitive market economy that was fully integrated into the global economic system. It had three core components: an ambitious program to reduce the government's chronic budget deficits by cutting government services and subsidies; liberalization of interest rates and the exchange rate, which meant that the government could no longer manipulate these rates to maintain political and social stability; and a sweeping program of privatization to sell state-owned firms to private investors.

These commitments led to important structural changes. The government reduced public investment dramatically. It also cut subsidies from 5.2 percent of GDP in 1992 to 1.6 percent in 1997, which entailed sharply reducing the number of items subsidized from 18 to 4 (bread, wheat flour, sugar, and cooking oil). The government also embarked on an extensive privatization program. As the economist Khalid Ikram observes, "Privatization on the scale proposed was not simply a financial exercise, but rather the abandonment of a model of development that has shaped Egyptian society for a generation."[7] In the early 1990s, state-owned enterprises still produced around 10 percent of GDP and employed about 12 percent of the labor force. They operated in virtually every sector of the economy from industrial raw materials (iron, steel, cement, phosphates) to consumer goods (refrigerators, soap, beer) to services (hotels, movies). They also dominated the banking and insurance sectors. In July 1991, the government began to privatize 314 of these state-owned enterprises. By June 2000, it had sold a controlling interest in 118 enterprises with a sale value of about 12.3 billion LE. In 1998, the IMF concluded that Egypt's privatization program was the fourth most successful in the world.[8]

By the mid-1990s, implementation of the structural adjustment program had produced significant improvements in Egypt's macroeconomic situation. The contrast between 1990 and 1996 was dramatic: GDP growth went from negative 2 percent to positive 5 percent; inflation fell from over 20 percent to 7 percent; the government budget deficit fell from 20 percent of GDP to 2 percent; savings rose from 8 percent of GDP to 19 percent; the current account deficit fell; and, the country's foreign exchange reserves rose from US$3 billion to US$17 billion. New laws governing labor relations, property rights, formation of companies, capital markets, and banking began to shift Egypt toward a more competitive and market-oriented economy. It joined the World Trade Organization and announced plans to participate in the Euro-Mediterranean free-trade zone.

With the adoption of these wide-ranging reforms, the government abandoned the Nasserist doctrine of state-guided economic development and guarantees of subsidized food, transportation, clothing, and energy. In an important sense, the regime became hollow. It had renounced the ideology on which it was based and the principles that gave it legitimacy. This development did not, in itself, constitute an immediate threat to regime stability. Indeed, the improved economic performance resulting from the reforms of the 1990s probably enhanced the regime's strength. However, by abandoning any pretense of upholding the basic premises of Nasserism, the regime lost its ideological legitimacy. Its legitimacy was now grounded entirely in its economic performance. Its impressive economic statistics reflected meaningful improvements in overall economic performance, but these gains were distributed unevenly. Elites with the right connections and skills thrived in the new economy. Those without these advantages—such as workers in state-owned enterprises, civil servants, and peasants—fell behind quickly. These groups, which had been the core supporters of the Nasserist regime and still expected the Nasserist social contract to be fulfilled, grew angry and disillusioned. This anger and disillusionment helped to fuel the 2011 uprising.

How Did the Military's Role Change under Sadat and Mubarak?

As mentioned earlier, Nasser began moving the military out of politics and domestic security after the 1967 war. Sadat continued this path, ostensibly to allow the military to focus on recovering the Sinai Peninsula from Israel but also to ensure that the military could not pose a threat to his power. In November 1971, Sadat granted himself de facto control over military promotions. In 1973, he was the key figure in determining Egypt's military strategy during the October war with Israel. He pursued a strategy that was deeply controversial within the military. He calculated that Egypt could not defeat Israel, particularly in light of the broad US commitment to Israel's security. His goal during the war was not to inflict maximum injury on Israel or even to expel Israeli forces from Sinai. Rather, his objective was to demonstrate to the Israelis that he had the military capacity to inflict significant damage and, thus, they should negotiate a permanent peace. He also hoped to show the United States that the continuation of the Arab-Israeli conflict destabilized the entire region and warranted more intensive American efforts to find a solution. In Sadat's words, his goal was a "limited war" that would use military force to facilitate these political objectives.

Egypt's senior generals sharply disagreed. During the first few days of the war, their forces were surprisingly successful. The military command called on Sadat to build on these victories and push the Israelis out of Sinai. Sadat declined and instead held his forces back. This step allowed the Israelis to regroup and eventually counterattack, leading to an ambiguous outcome—Egyptian troops had crossed the Suez Canal and held territory in Sinai, but Israeli troops had cut them off from their supply lines and were in a position to attack Cairo. As discussed below, this situation set in motion a series of negotiations that culminated in the 1979 peace treaty between Israel and Egypt. However, Sadat's decision to squander the early victories of the 1973 war made him deeply unpopular with senior generals. Sadat dismissed their concerns on the grounds that they lacked the vision to see his broader political objective, which was to regain the Sinai Peninsula through a peace treaty that ended the conflict with Israel and solidified Egypt's relationship with the United States. His military critics asserted that he had betrayed the brave soldiers who sacrificed their lives and then entered into a flawed negotiating process where Israel held all the cards and the United States consistently backed the Israelis. Sadat became alienated from the senior military leadership and sought to further decrease their political influence. He also redirected the armed forces from combat toward economic and civilian projects, partly to help develop the country and partly to ensure that no military leader had the prominence to challenge him.[9]

As a counterweight to the military, Sadat dramatically expanded the size of the Ministry of Interior (MOI) and gave it broad responsibility for domestic security. He staffed it with officers whom he trusted and enhanced its capacity to investigate any threats to the state. The MOI was given authority to screen applicants for membership in the ruling NDP; to monitor and weaken anti-NDP forces in universities, factories, and villages; and to rig parliamentary, student, and syndicate elections to guarantee NDP victories. The ministry's intelligence branch also monitored the military and had the authority to disqualify candidates for military promotion. In addition, senior police generals were appointed as provincial governors, in order to further enhance the ministry's influence at the local level. [10]

Despite these efforts to strengthen the MOI, it still lacked the capacity to contain large-scale demonstrations. This limitation became apparent in 1977 when Sadat faced large riots sparked by a sharp increase in the price of bread. The MOI's forces were unable to handle the situation, and Sadat had no choice but to call on the military to restore order. His central lesson from this experience was to further strengthen the MOI by increasing its rank and file and acquiring more equipment. The United States played an important role in equipping this enhanced security force.[11]

The military leadership reportedly resented the diversion of resources and power to the MOI. However, they could do little about it. The tensions between Sadat and the military led to speculation that some elements of the military may have been involved in Sadat's assassination in 1981. In the wake of the assassination, the MOI rounded up a wide range of suspects including several military officers.[12]

Mubarak assumed power at a time when the military was deemed politically unreliable and the MOI had acted decisively to defend the regime. Thus, even though Mubarak came from the military (he was a former commander of the air force), he continued the policy of strengthening the MOI and minimizing the military's political role. He expanded the appointment of former police officers to senior political positions in the cabinet and in the governing council of the ruling party. He also dramatically increased the number of soldiers under the control of the MOI. Soldiers directly employed by the ministry rose to 1 million by 2002, an increase from 9 percent to 21 percent of state employment in 28 years. The military, by comparison, had no more than 460,000 men. The budget of the MOI increased from 3.5 percent of GDP to almost 6 percent between 1988 and 2002.[13]

Both the Central Security Forces and the police forces were deployed extensively in the state's clash with militant Islamist groups during the late 1990s. The insurgency was eventually repressed, but human rights abuses were rampant. Several scholars have argued that the reliance on torture that emerged within the security services during this period spread to police relations with ordinary citizens. Getting hauled into the local police station often meant enduring torture. The most frequent victims of police abuse were not political dissidents but poor citizens without influential connections. Corruption within the police force also became widespread. The growing brutality and abuse by the police contributed to the widespread public anger that led to the 2011 uprising.

In addition, the security forces under Mubarak increasingly contracted with *baltigayya*, or thugs, as part of a broader pattern of cooperation with organized criminal networks. Thugs were hired to inform on Egyptians, infiltrate and disrupt protests, and carry out other activities for the MOI or the government's NDP. The connections forged between some members of the police and these criminal networks proved difficult to unravel after 2011.[14]

While Mubarak expanded the power and resources of the MOI, he still needed to retain the support of the military. In broad terms, there were two components to his strategy. First, he provided the military with a steady flow of new and complex equipment from the United States, purchased with American military aid. The military then focused its attention on learning how to use this equipment, deploy it, and integrate it into its strategy. Second, he allowed the military to expand its role in the civilian economy. For the reasons mentioned earlier, Mubarak was both unable and unwilling to significantly increase the budget for the military. However, he needed to ensure that the officer corps enjoyed a comfortable standard of living and were willing to acquiesce to the regime. He achieved these goals by permitting the military to broaden its network of economic enterprises.

As mentioned earlier, the military's role in the civilian economy had grown sharply under Sadat. It grew even further under Mubarak. Military firms became major players in construction, land reclamation, agriculture, and a host of other activities. They produced a wide range of goods including clothing, foodstuffs, kitchen appliances, and automobiles. In addition, officers were granted discounted apartments and vacation homes, subsidized food and services, and opportunities for lucrative appointments in the state-owned sector after retirement. [15]

Did Egypt Make Progress toward Democracy under Sadat and Mubarak?

Political scientists make a distinction between political liberalization and democratization. Liberalization entails an improvement in civil and political liberties such as freedom of expression, freedom of the press, and freedom of assembly. However, these changes fall short of democratization, which involves progress toward selecting the leadership of the country through competitive elections in which virtually all adults may vote and run for office.

During the Sadat and Mubarak eras, Egypt saw meaningful political liberalization in several areas. These included multiparty political competition for Parliament; increased judicial independence, which led to judicial rulings that reined in some abuses by the executive; a rise in the number of civil society groups that enabled citizens to organize around shared concerns; an expansion in the political role of professional associations, which commented regularly on government policy; periods of greater press freedom, which, at times, included sharp criticism of the government; and the emergence of human rights groups, which, while often facing harassment from the regime, were permitted to function for most of the 1980s, 1990s, and 2000s. There were limits in each of these areas, however. New parties had to be approved by a parliamentary committee controlled by the ruling party and could not organize at the local level. The judiciary was eventually reined in through appointments of quiescent judges to senior posts and through pressuring its budget. Non-governmental organizations, professional associations, and human rights groups operated under the constant threat of government interference and, on occasion, closure. Despite these limits, Egypt was a freer place under Sadat and Mubarak than it was under Nasser.

However, Egypt was not a democracy and showed few signs of developing into one. Power was still tightly concentrated in the executive branch and, particularly, the president. For most of this period, the president was chosen by the NDP-controlled Parliament and then approved by the public in carefully managed national referenda that routinely returned overwhelming "yes" votes. As noted earlier, the one exception to this pattern was an ostensibly competitive election for president in 2005 that returned Mubarak to power with 88 percent of the vote. Parliament was selected in similarly managed elections that always produced a victory for the ruling NDP. Furthermore, Parliament played only a minor role in actually producing legislation. Most laws emanated from the executive and were quickly approved by a compliant Parliament.

One of the interesting features of the regime during this period was its use of parliamentary elections. These carefully managed elections reflected a strategy of authoritarian control, rather than progress toward democracy. Elections served several functions. First, they provided a means for assessing the competence and loyalty of party cadres. The Mubarak regime found particular utility in pitting the NDP candidate in a district against independent candidates, who were typically businessmen or local notables. If the independent did well, he/she would be invited to join the NDP, thereby ensuring

that the NDP was co-opting those individuals who could deliver meaningful support at the local level. Elections were also
useful for evaluating the opposition. They enabled the regime
to identify the districts where the opposition enjoyed support
and then either deny those districts state resources or develop
a strategy to entice them into the government's camp. In addition, elections provided a means for signaling the regime's
strength. The NDP was more effective if the party could persuade elites that it commanded vast resources and broad mobilization capability—and, therefore, was a powerful ally who
could reward its friends and punish its enemies. Through
large victories, the NDP demonstrated its power and thereby
consolidated the elite coalition that underlay the regime. Even
if these victories were facilitated by violence and fraud, they
still served the political purpose of demonstrating that the NDP
could control the political arena, reliably place its supporters
in Parliament, and assure them the opportunity to profit while
enjoying immunity from legal prosecution. However, even this
system had its limits. In the parliamentary elections of 2010, the
party's leadership engaged in electoral abuse on an unprece-
dented scale in order to gain complete control of Parliament
and lay the groundwork for Hosni Mubarak's son to ascend to
the presidency. The scope of this abuse was outrageous even
by the standards of Mubarak's Egypt and deepened the public
anger that culminated in the 2011 uprising.[16]

Suggested Readings

For a detailed analysis of the 1952 coup, see Joel Gordon, *Nasser's
   Blessed Movement* (Oxford, 1992). Gordon has also written a concise
   biography of Nasser, *Nasser: Hero of the Arab Nation* (Oneworld,
   2006). For an insider's view of this period, try any of the books by
   Mohamed Heikel: *Sphinx and Commissar* (Collins, 1978); *The Road to
   Ramadan* (Quadrangle, 1975); or *Autumn of Fury* (Random House,
   1983). For Sadat's view, see his autobiography, *In Search of Identity*
   (Harper Collins, 1978). For further information on Sadat, consult
   the fine biography by Robert L. Tignor, *Anwar al-Sadat: Transforming*

the Middle East (Oxford, 2016). For a thoughtful scholar's perspective based on extensive interviews with retired leaders from the Nasser and Sadat eras, see Kirk J. Beattie's *Egypt during the Nasser Years* (Westview, 1994) and *Egypt during the Sadat Years* (Palgrave, 2000). For an insightful discussion of the competing visions of Egypt's future in the late Sadat/early Mubarak period, see Raymond William Baker, *Sadat and After* (Harvard, 1990). For analysis of political economy issues, the two best studies are John Waterbury, *The Egypt of Nasser and Sadat: The Political Economy of Two Regimes* (Princeton, 1993) and Khalid Ikram, *The Egyptian Economy, 1952–2000* (Routledge, 2006). For the perspective of one of Egypt's most respected economists, see Galal Amin, *Egypt's Economic Predicament* (E.J. Brill, 1995) and *Egypt in the Era of Hosni Mubarak* (American University in Cairo, 2011). Amin has also written two lighthearted and insightful books on the period: *Whatever Happened to the Egyptians?* and *Whatever Else Happened to the Egyptians?*, both with the American University in Cairo Press. For analysis of the Mubarak era, try Robert Springborg, *Mubarak's Egypt: Fragmentation of the Political Order* (Westview, 1989) and Eberhard Kienle, *A Grand Delusion: Democracy and Economic Reform in Egypt* (I.B. Tauris, 2001). For an assessment of politics at the end of Mubarak's rule, see Bruce K. Rutherford, *Egypt after Mubarak: Liberalism, Islam, and Democracy in the Arab World* (Princeton, 2008). For discussion of the military and the internal security apparatus, see Hazem Kandil, *Soldiers, Spies, and Statesmen* (Verso, 2012). For a fascinating portrayal of Egyptian society in the late Mubarak period by one of Egypt's most respected novelists, try Alaa al-Aswany, *The Yacoubian Building* (Harper, 2006). This novel has also been made into a film with English subtitles that is available on DVD and some streaming video services.

4

ECONOMIC DEVELOPMENT AND HUMAN WELFARE

What Is Egypt's Level of Human Development?

For many decades, national development was measured in terms of simplistic economic indicators such as gross national product (GNP). Several scholars challenged these measures in the 1970s. Amartya Sen, Mahbub al-Haq, Martha Nussbaum, and others argued that human well-being is less about aggregate economic growth and more about whether individuals and families have access to adequate food, health, education, civil and human rights, and decent employment. Development should enhance capacities and opportunity as well as income. Thus, the human development perspective placed rights— human, social, and economic—at the center of debates about what constitutes economic development.

The first Human Development Index (HDI) was published in 1990 by the United Nations Development Programme (UNDP). It includes life expectancy at birth, expected and mean years of schooling, and gross national income per capita.[1] In 2016, UNDP ranked Egypt 111 out of 188 countries, classifying it as a lower middle income country. Egypt's ranking was the same as that of Turkmenistan, a sparsely populated former Soviet republic in Central Asia. The ranking was also three spots lower than it had been in 2010, the year before the 2011 uprising.

Egypt's relatively poor ranking does not mean that progress on improving health and income has been absent. In the

25 years between the publication of the first HDI in 1990 and the 2015 HDI, many Egyptians became better off.[2] The average Egyptian born in 1990 could expect to live 64.6 years; in 2015, average life expectancy was 71.3 years, slightly higher than for the Middle East as a whole. Egyptians completed 7.1 years of school on average, up from only 3.5 years. Gross national income per person almost doubled, from US$5,869 per person to US$10,064 (measured in 2011 purchasing power parity).

This was not a steady increase in living standards, however. Egypt experienced volatility and economic crises, and the gains from economic growth were not distributed evenly. Wars and conflicts in the Middle East also dampened economic growth and trade, and disrupted the opportunities for Egyptians to work in other Arab countries and send funds home to their families. Real wages (wages adjusted for inflation) declined between 1988 and 1998, rose between 1998 and 2006, but then were stagnant through 2012. Periods of high inflation further eroded the ability of Egyptians to buy what they need. In addition, as Egypt's population has grown, the state has lacked the resources to provide adequate public services to all its citizens. Growing poverty, inadequate diets, high pollution, and poor quality healthcare have contributed to a steady decline in the quality of life for many Egyptians.

How Many Egyptians Are Poor?

Poverty is one of Egypt's gravest problems. Egypt's statistical agency, the Central Agency for Public Mobilization and Statistics (CAPMAS), reported in 2016 that 27.8 percent of the population fell below the official poverty line, that is, were living on less than $2.20 per day.[3] More Egyptians were living in poverty than in 1995, when 22.9 percent of the population fell below the national poverty line. Another 23.7 percent of Egyptians were classified as "near-poor" in 2011, with monthly incomes near or just above the poverty line.

The number of poor people increased during the last few years of Mubarak's tenure, particularly after the global financial crisis in 2008 and the rise in global food prices in 2010. The average Egyptian spends over 40 percent of his or her income on food. Thus, food price shocks tend to push many vulnerable households deeper into poverty. One of the most important challenges for the al-Sisi government has been bringing down inflation and arresting the sharp decline in value of the Egyptian pound, which left many more Egyptians living precariously than before the 2011/2012 uprising.

Geographic location, years of schooling, and family size all impact who is poor. Poverty is geographically concentrated in Upper (southern) Egypt and in rural areas, with increasing pockets of urban poverty as well. In 2015, the government reported that 56.7 percent of Egyptians were poor in Upper Egypt, versus 19.7 percent in the Nile Delta and 18 percent in Cairo. National statistics regularly undercount the urban poor, however, as any visitor to Cairo's extensive informal urban slums can attest. A 2013 World Food Program report found that between 2009 and 2011 poverty in urban areas increased by 40 percent. In the Greater Cairo urban area alone, approximately 3.8 million people are classified as poor, more than in any other province in Egypt.[4]

Many poor Egyptians also suffer from malnutrition, with children particularly hard hit. In 2011, half of all children under five suffered from anemia, while 31 percent were stunted. In addition, government subsidies for food and other items do not reach all poor households, and tend to disproportionately benefit the better-off among Egyptian society. In a 2011 survey, 19 percent of poor households did not have access to a ration card with which to purchase subsidized food. Egypt's 2016 agreement with the IMF that provides the government with short-term loans includes goals of building a stronger social safety net to better address malnutrition and food insecurity.

How Unequal Is Egypt? What Types of Inequality Matter in Egypt?

Public discontent during the Mubarak era was driven in part by both perceived and actual increases in inequality. But what kinds of inequality matter in Egypt? The conventional measure of inequality is based on the distribution of income (typically captured by the Gini coefficient, where 0 represents perfect equality and 100 perfect inequality). Egypt's Gini coefficient of 30.8 puts the country at 130 out of 154 countries around the world in terms of income inequality, meaning there are great divides between rich and poor. However, this level of income inequality is typical of many poor developing countries and some industrialized countries as well.

More adequate measures of inequality focus on what is called inequality of opportunity—how much access to education, employment, and income depends upon factors outside of an individual's or household's control. On these measures, Egypt demonstrates significant and rising inequality. Advantaged families are able to obtain education and jobs for their children at much higher rates than children from disadvantaged families. When the HDI is weighted for inequalities in opportunities to access healthcare, education, and income, Egypt performs poorly, losing 29 percent of its HDI value. Egypt's "loss" of human well-being due to inequalities in education and healthcare is very similar to that incurred by Morocco and is a slightly higher loss than for the Arab countries as a whole.

Economic inequality in Egypt is closely tied to the geographic distribution of poverty and stems from neglect by the central government of the provinces. As in the United States and many other countries, the place where one lives has a significant impact on one's life chances. In Egypt, residents in large urban areas such as Cairo, Alexandria, and Suez have better access to employment, education, and healthcare. Residents in Upper (southern) Egypt have long had significantly worse measures of human development than those in the Nile Delta. Within Upper Egypt, people living in cities and larger towns fare better than those in villages.

Economic marginalization in the Sinai Peninsula, where 70 percent of the population are indigenous Bedouin, is severe. Official development statistics often simply exclude the Bedouin population altogether. North Sinai is ranked as the poorest province in Egypt, while other parts of Sinai also suffer from grinding poverty. The government's sporadic efforts to develop Sinai have focused on attracting Egyptians from the Nile Valley to the area, and have paid little attention to generating employment and building infrastructure for the local population. For example, under Mubarak, the government facilitated the development of many tourist resorts in South Sinai by well-connected businessmen and retired officers from the army and police. Tourism development thus largely benefited investors from the Nile Valley and temporary workers who came to work in the resorts, excluding local Bedouin communities.

Rural-urban disparities also emerge when considering infant mortality rates. Infant mortality is higher in rural areas than the national average and higher among low-income families, many of whom live in Upper Egypt. Mortality rates for children under five show a sharp rural-urban disparity, with 34 children out of 1,000 dying before the age of five in rural areas, in contrast to 23 children dying out of 1,000 in urban areas.

Geography as a source of inequality reflects historical patterns of unequal development and inadequate governmental attempts to address these patterns. For example, as Ellis Goldberg has argued, the cultivation and harvest of cotton in Upper Egypt during the nineteenth and early twentieth centuries relied on the extensive use of child labor. Children and families thus became the primary workers on the cotton and sugar estates in Egypt. Estate owners, merchants, and shareholders saw little need to diversify economic activity in Upper Egypt away from cotton and sugar, or promote literacy among their young workers.[5] These cruel legacies remain evident in the socioeconomic marginalization of these areas.

What Explains Egypt's Growing Population?

Egypt is the 16th most populous country in the world, with the largest population in the Arab world and the third largest in Africa, after Ethiopia and Nigeria. In 2017, the country was home to approximately 95 million people, growing by roughly 1 million persons every six months, with most of this growth in Cairo and other urban areas.[6] When Nasser took power in 1952, Egypt's population was approximately 22.2 million. The population doubled by 1981 and more than doubled again by 2015, when it reached 88 million. In the 10 years between 2006 and 2016 alone, Egypt added 20 million people—a number roughly equal to the entire population of Syria and twice the population of Jordan. Egypt's growth rate is significantly higher than some other developing countries, particularly China and India, but is similar to that of Pakistan and Nigeria.

According to Egyptian government statistics, the population growth rate was 2.75 percent annually between 1976 and 1986. It fell to roughly 2 percent annually from 1986 to 2006, but after the 2008 global economic crisis and 2011 uprising, it rose to 2.55 percent. The total fertility rate—the number of children that Egyptian women have on average—increased to 3.5 children per woman by 2014 after remaining stagnant at around 3 children per woman between 1995 and 2005. Not all of these children were wanted. Forty-six percent of women with four children reported they would have preferred fewer children, while 66 percent of those with five children reported unwanted pregnancies.[7]

As in many developing countries, these demographic trends have produced a "youth bulge." In 2014, roughly 57 percent of the Egyptian population was under the age of 25 and 35.3 percent was under the age of 15. This means that nonworking children are a significantly larger share of the population in Egypt than in many other countries, placing a large burden on those of working age. Economic growth has not kept pace with the number of people seeking decent employment, and the rapid expansion in population outstrips the state's capacity to provide public services and infrastructure.

Egypt's population since 2011 has also been augmented by refugees fleeing from wars in Libya and elsewhere in the region. The United Nations refugee agency (UNHCR) registered over 232,000 refugees in Egypt as of May 2018, primarily from Syria. However, most refugees in Egypt remain unregistered and undocumented, with no formal access to protections under international refugee law.

In general, fertility rates—the number of children borne by the average woman—decrease as women gain stronger legal rights, more education, job opportunities, and affordable access to healthcare and family planning services. Many of the social policies that improve gender equality and economic productivity of women also contribute to smaller families. Public and political support for sexuality education, family planning, and women's rights thus matter greatly in limiting rates of population increase. How do Egyptian women fare in terms of the factors that affect fertility?

Legal rights: In Egypt's legal system, the laws that regulate marriage, divorce, inheritance, and child custody—termed family status law—depend upon a person's religious affiliation. For the approximately 90 percent of Egyptians who identify as Sunni Muslims, family status law draws upon understandings of Islamic law, which can change over time. Social norms and expectations also play an important role in determining family size. Marriage in Egypt is a good example. Three out of four women over the age of 16 in Egypt are married. Many women still marry at a relatively early age; the median age of marriage in 2014 was 21 years. While the government has raised the legal age of marriage to 18, it remains highly socially desirable in Egypt that marriages result promptly in children. Most married women thus give birth to their first child in their first or second year of marriage.

Divorce laws have been slowly changing but remain highly discriminatory toward women. Muslim men in Egypt can divorce their wives without recourse to the courts, but women must still use family courts to end a marriage. Coptic Christians can only be granted divorce by the Coptic Church, which strictly limits the grounds for divorce. Egyptian attitudes toward divorce have become more accepting, particularly among young women. However, many women remain unaware of their rights or are unable to pursue them, particularly in poor and rural areas. Men and women also differ in their views about further legal changes for women's rights. For instance, on the issue of whether Egypt should pass a law criminalizing domestic violence and marital rape, a 2017 UN survey found that while 70 percent of women supported it, only 45 percent of men did.[8]

Education: Egypt has increased educational opportunities for girls and boys alike since the 1960s, when Nasser's government invested in the rapid expansion of educational opportunity. As of 2015, over 98 percent of children attended primary school. For Egyptians under the age of 25, the expected years of education are virtually the same for boys and girls, with both genders expected to complete 13 years of schooling. Girls currently spend slightly more time, on average, in school than boys. However, the situation is different for older cohorts of women, many of whom are still in their childbearing years. Only 54.5 percent of women over 25 have some secondary schooling (beyond primary school), in contrast to 68.2 percent of their male counterparts. Illiteracy among adults, particularly women, thus remains high. A quarter of all Egyptian women are illiterate, with older, poorer women in rural areas the least likely to have had access to education.

Employment: Multiple studies have found that women who engage in paid work are more empowered in household decision-making, have fewer children, space their children out more, and are more likely to use modern family planning methods. Egypt performs quite poorly on cross-national rankings of women in the labor force. It ranked 132 out of 144 countries in the 2016 World Economic Forum Gender Gap Index.[9] Only 18 percent of women aged 15–64 were working in a wage-earning job in 2012, whereas 77 percent of men were employed. For younger women aged 15–35, paid jobs are even less likely—only 15 percent were in the labor force as of 2014.

Why are women employed outside the home at far lower rates than men? Family and social expectations, job scarcity, and competing demands on women's time from household chores and childrearing combine to keep many women from working. Attitudes toward women in the labor force are changing but in many cases still reflect conventional expectations that women will handle household duties while men work outside the home to provide for the family.[10] In a 2017 UN-Promundo survey, 68% of Egyptian women thought that women should prioritize marriage over career, as did 73% of men.[11] Thus marriage itself serves as a turning point for many women. Those working in the private and informal sectors are less likely to work after marriage. Whether they work or not, women remain the primary caregivers for children and are primarily responsible for household work.

Many women prefer public sector jobs because they are generally viewed as more stable and provide some benefits and protections, even though the salaries are generally very poor. The wage gap between men and women is also considerably less in the government and public sector than in the private sector. However, the number of public sector jobs has been shrinking over the past few decades as the government tried to reduce its wage bill in the face of chronic budget deficits. This development has meant that fewer women find work in state agencies and public sector enterprises.

Healthcare and contraceptive access: The Egyptian government invested heavily in expanding healthcare during the Nasser period. As with other public services, dense patterns of urbanization facilitated extending basic healthcare services to many Egyptians and produced some significant improvements in the health of women and children. For instance, infant mortality in Egypt declined from 63 deaths per 1,000 live births in 1995 to 22 deaths per 1,000 live births in 2014. A skilled attendant participates in 80 percent of births, and as a result maternal mortality rates have consistently fallen over time.

Despite the expansion of healthcare, there is a significant unmet demand for contraception and family planning services. Only 59 percent of all childbearing women reported using contraceptives in 2017. As with other public services, low-income families and those living in Upper Egypt and in rural areas have less access to family planning services and healthcare than the more urbanized areas of the Nile Delta. Contraceptive use in the Nile Delta, for instance, is above 62 percent for currently married women, but only 46.7 percent of married women in rural Upper Egypt use contraceptives.[12]

There is ample evidence that Egypt can implement targeted public health interventions successfully. For example, to lower maternal and infant mortality rates, the Ministry of Health upgraded maternity and postnatal clinics in the 1990s. This program sought to provide adequate care for delivery and follow-up, as well as referrals to hospitals for complicated pregnancies. As a result, Egypt significantly decreased the number of children dying before the age of five, from 85 children per 1,000 live births in 1990 to 22 children in 2013. Maternal mortality rates—where women die in childbirth—also decreased. An average of 120 women died in childbirth per 100,000 live births in 1990, but in 2013, this figure had decreased to 45 deaths per 100,000 live births.[13]

What Additional Factors Affect the Status of Women in Egypt?

On the United Nations Gender Inequality Index, where 1 is the best score, Egypt ranks quite poorly, scoring 131 among 155 countries. Women's life expectancy at birth in Egypt is higher than that of men, but they have fewer opportunities for employment and weaker protection of basic rights than men. As we saw in the previous question, exclusion from employment opportunities, social expectations of early marriage, and inadequate access to contraceptives limit women's empowerment and contribute to large family size with many children. In addition to the socioeconomic and health dimensions of gender inequality discussed previously, women's status is also affected by the extent of violence within the family, public opinion about women's rights, and the role of the state in inflicting gender-specific forms of violence.

Gender-based violence within the family is extensive and disproportionately affects women in Egypt. Domestic violence, primarily by husbands against wives, affected roughly 40 percent of households surveyed by UN Promundo in 2017. In addition, female genital mutilation (FGM) is widely practiced, with the government reporting that 92 percent of currently or formerly married women between the ages of 15 and 49 had undergone the procedure. The Egyptian government formally outlawed FGM in 2008 and, in 2016, the Egyptian Parliament passed legislation imposing prison sentences on those performing the procedure or escorting girls to undergo it. However, since 2008, only one prosecution has occurred. Women's rights advocates argue that prevention and public awareness campaigns to change social norms are as important as criminalization. Some of these efforts have produced results and contributed to changing attitudes toward FGM. The 2015 Egyptian Health Issues Survey found that 40 percent of men and 46 percent of women surveyed did not support the practice.

Young Egyptians as a whole, however, do not necessarily hold more progressive views on women's empowerment overall than older generations. Several robust public opinion studies have found that majorities of young Egyptians hold traditional gender views that posit men as breadwinners and heads of household and women as wives and mothers. Majorities of youth also supported men's authority within the household, although young men hold these views more than young women do.

Education and class position profoundly shape aspirations for women and attitudes toward gender equality. Higher levels of education in Egypt—as in other countries—strongly correspond to more egalitarian gender views. Gender roles may also be changing as a result of the 2011 and 2013 cycles of mass mobilization. Middle class, educated young women played leading roles in the 2011 uprising by organizing online and in the streets, and women of all classes and backgrounds took part in the occupations of squares and public spaces. However, this widespread participation also generated a backlash, specifically from the military and security forces.

Organized episodes of sexual assault came to mark the public demonstrations and sit-ins. Many activists believed that some of these incidents were organized by thugs coordinated by the security forces. Female activists were specifically targeted in the 2011 uprising, particularly in the infamous episode where the army administered what it termed "virginity tests" to 18 female detainees. One of them, Samira Ibrahim, filed a lawsuit against the practice, and the Cairo Administrative Court eventually found these actions illegal. However, in 2012, a military court acquitted the military doctor who administered the tests. By 2014, human rights groups reported that the security forces and police were still using invasive "virginity tests" on detained female activists and prisoners.[14]

Are Egyptians Employed?

The Egyptian economy needs to generate hundreds of thousands of new jobs every year in order to absorb new entrants into the workforce and keep unemployment at the 12.5 percent rate reported by the National Bank of Egypt for 2016/2017. The official unemployment rate, however, is widely regarded as significantly understating the extent of unemployment and, more important, underemployment. Many Egyptians cannot find work commensurate with their skills and expectations. The jobs that they find are often in the informal sector, seasonal, and poorly paid. For instance, in surveys conducted by UN Women-Promundo, 85 percent of men reported that they were employed. Of these, 44 percent reported that their work was seasonal while another 40 percent said they spent most of their time out of work or looking for work. Many men thus had difficulty adequately providing for their families, leading over half of them to report stress and depression. The problem of youth unemployment is also particularly acute, as it is across the Arab world. Youth unemployment in Egypt remained over 30 percent in 2017.

Available jobs have shifted to less stable and less remunerative work in the informal sector. According to the International Labor Organization, informal work entails labor that is not recognized, recorded, protected, or regulated by the public authorities. The 2016 *Arab Human Development Report* (AHDR) noted that while in 1980, 16 percent of Egyptians worked in informal jobs, by 2000, 43 percent of Egyptians were in the informal sector.[15] Government employment surveys, using more restrictive methods for counting "informal" employment than those employed by the AHDR, reported 37 percent of men working informal jobs in 2012.[16]

The weak rate of job creation has several structural causes. The industrial sector contains dozens of large and inefficient state-owned firms that cannot compete on the global stage, although the public sector only represents 33 percent of GDP generated in Egypt. In addition, government ministries have created an extensive web of rules and regulations that insert state bureaucrats into virtually every aspect of business and systematically favor large firms over the enormous number of very small firms with fewer than 10 employees that account for most jobs. Small- and medium-sized firms, which have significant potential to create jobs, face enormous difficulties in acquiring the capital and permits needed to grow. Egypt is not alone in facing the challenge of creating decent jobs in the formal sector. The informalization of work and rising inequality between poor and rich are global phenomena, requiring rethinking of development strategies not just at the level of individual countries but regionally and globally as well.

What Economic Challenges Do Young People Face?

Egypt's "youth bulge" mirrors demographic trends across the Middle East and North Africa, where 30 percent of the region's population is between the ages of 15 and 29.[17] Many young people face what Diane Singerman and others have called the problem of "waithood." Because they cannot find employment, many young people do not have the financial means to afford basic housing, enter into marriage, or achieve other markers of adulthood in Egyptian society.[18] Attaining higher levels of education does not ensure employment, as many youth with high school and college degrees cannot find jobs. Informal employment for first-time job entrants has become the norm. In the early 2000s, three-quarters of people entering the labor market for the first time took informal jobs.[19]

Youth also face difficulties in establishing their own households because of the high cost of housing. Many Egyptians must spend more of their household income on housing than families in developed countries. Housing prices in turn reflect the scarcity of affordable housing. The World Bank estimates that the country faces a shortfall of 3.5 million homes and that between 12 million and 20 million Egyptians

live in informal housing—that is, housing that is unregistered with local authorities and/or is not compliant with local
zoning, construction, and safety regulations. The housing
shortage and poor quality of much informal housing has important repercussions for young people trying to start families.
As young men reach marriageable age, many cannot afford a
decent apartment, traditionally a precondition for marriage
in Egypt.

Many youth in Egypt are excluded from opportunities to
further their education or to pursue work. The Population
Council conducted a survey of 10,916 Egyptian youth, defined broadly as 15–30 years old, in 2014.[20] Of those surveyed,
40.7 percent were not involved in education, employment, or
training programs of any kind. Young women in rural areas
from poor families were disproportionately represented in this
group of marginalized youths. Of those surveyed, 69.7 percent of women were not involved in any form of education,
employment, or training. (This figure includes those who reported that they were housewives, which was not counted
as a type of unpaid employment.) More than half of women
living in rural areas who were not involved in work or education also did not have a secondary education. In contrast,
only 13 percent of men in urban areas and 10 percent of men in
rural areas reported that they did not participate in education,
work, or training. The highest rates of youth marginalization
were in provinces (governorates) that depend upon tourism
as the principal source of employment. Tourism suffered
steep declines after 2011 and was further hit as the conflict between ISIS affiliates and the al-Sisi government intensified in
Sinai after 2013. Young men living in urban areas also faced
problems finding a place in the economy: 50 percent held a
university degree but were still not able to participate in work,
education, or training.

The pool of young people with little economic opportunity
grows steadily each year. At the same time, improvements
in communication technology—particularly, access to the

internet, social media, and satellite television—enable young people to see the better quality of life enjoyed in other countries, which leads to rising expectations that the current economic system is largely unable to fulfill. As a result, many talented youth seek education and employment abroad.

In the past, many young people traveled to the Arab states of the Persian Gulf to work. However, these opportunities are drying up. Fluctuating oil prices in the oil-rich Gulf States have limited government investment in big projects. These governments also face pressures to increase employment for their citizens, rather than hire foreigners. At the same time, young Egyptians face growing obstacles to work and education in Europe and the US due to growing political pressures to limit immigration.

Is Egypt Urbanizing? Which Cities Are Most Important?

Cities and towns are growing rapidly in Egypt. While Egypt is a large country, most of its territory is made up of desert and mountains and only 8 percent is inhabited. Population density in the Nile Valley and Nile Delta is thus among the highest in the world, at 1,136.5 persons per square kilometer in 2016. For decades, the government's neglect of the agricultural sector and the provision of better public services in urban areas led many Egyptians to leave smaller villages in Upper Egypt and in the Nile Delta for larger urban areas. Most rural migrants moved to rapidly growing informal urban areas (ashwiya'at) in and around Egypt's two largest cities, Cairo and Alexandria.

Cairo is the largest city in the Middle East and North Africa and historically has been one of the most important urban centers in the Middle East. In Egyptian colloquial Arabic, it is referred to as Umm al-Dunya, "mother of the world." The metropolitan area of Greater Cairo, including the provinces of Giza, Cairo, and Qalubiyya, is currently one of the great megacities of the developing world with a population of 22.9 million people in 2016. Greater Cairo is thus vastly larger than any US or European city and larger than the entire population of Syria. As the center of Egypt's economy, politics, culture, and government, Greater Cairo draws migrants from all over Egypt. Egyptians also move in smaller numbers to Alexandria, Egypt's second largest city. Alexandria is only a third the size of Cairo but both cities are ranked among the fastest growing in the world.

Generally, burgeoning informal areas in Cairo, Alexandria and other urban areas consist of compact, high-density settlements that offer affordable but substandard housing as well as employment opportunities in the informal sector. This unplanned, dense urbanization has minimized wasteful land use and facilitated residents' efforts to access basic public services. Although the government ignored and neglected these areas in its formal planning efforts, residents living in informal areas tapped into existing water and electricity grids, established extensive systems of private transport, and set up many small workshops and service activities. Millions of Egyptians have thus managed to obtain some employment and services for themselves in the face of great obstacles.[21]

Faced with this rapid and unplanned urbanization, governmental authorities generally have not razed informal housing areas, fearing social protest. There are well-known exceptions, including cases in Cairo where residents were displaced in favor of luxury towers and upscale shopping malls. More commonly, however, municipal and central authorities have retroactively recognized the largest informal areas and gradually extended electricity, water, and sanitation networks to parts of them, though many remain without adequate sewage connections. To limit demand for urban services, the government sometimes does not reclassify areas from "rural" to "urban" regardless of how many people live there. So-called rural villages in the Nile Delta, for instance, may include 10,000 to 20,000 people or more.[22]

Greater Cairo has steadily expanded into the surrounding irrigated and desert areas over the past few decades. Much of this growth comes at the expense of Egypt's limited amount of arable land, as irrigated fields near big cities and villages are converted every year to residential, commercial, and industrial uses. The Egyptian government has a long-standing ban on converting irrigated land to urban use and has mandated that all new development take place in the surrounding desert. However, the government has neither the capacity nor the will to enforce this rule adequately, nor is it clear that the ban makes much sense given the declining share of agriculture in the country's economy. Meanwhile, Cairo's desert outskirts increasingly host defense and security facilities, industrial zones, quarries, and an expanding number of satellite cities. Many better-off Egyptians have moved to these satellite cities, which are seen as less crowded and polluted, but are often distant from jobs and extended family networks.[23]

In central Cairo and Alexandria, dense urbanization was accompanied by an almost complete lack of green spaces and parks. In Cairo, public squares, green spaces along the Nile, irrigated fields, and private villa gardens disappeared rapidly over the course of the last few decades. Landowners and contractors found that they could make more money by constructing apartment buildings than by engaging in other land uses, while governmental authorities have made little investment in public parks.[24] One exception to this trend is a well-conceived redevelopment of an old garbage dump on the hills overlooking the medieval district of Cairo. The resulting Al Azhar Park, funded by the Aga Khan, shows how progressive urban planning for green spaces can help cool the city, reduce air pollution, and enhance the daily life of Cairo's millions of inhabitants.

Do Egyptians Have Access to Water, Sanitation, and Electricity?

Access to safe drinking water, adequate sanitation, and reliable electricity protects health and enables people to have productive working lives. Unequal access to these resources contributes to inequalities in health, economic productivity, and family well being. In Egypt, the dense patterns of urbanization described before facilitated providing electricity, water, and sewage services to most of the population, even as inequities in quality and coverage persist.

Unlike many developing countries, Egypt is almost fully electrified, with 99 percent of Egyptians having access to electricity. Particularly in the hot summer months, access to electricity for refrigeration, fans, and air conditioning is essential to human health. However, population growth, increased consumption, and inadequate investment in production and distribution systems strained Egypt's ability to supply adequate electricity during the 2000s. Rolling blackouts and power rationing became a frequent occurrence, particularly after 2012, contributing to a sharp decline in the popularity of then-president Muhammad Mursi and the Muslim Brotherhood. While the state-owned utilities pointed to technical problems of supply, many Brotherhood supporters believed that the electricity shortages were engineered by their opponents in an attempt to discredit them.

Water and sanitation accesses have also improved for many Egyptians but the quality and coverage are uneven across regions and parts of the population. By 2015, the government and the UN reported that 99 percent of Egyptians had access to an improved water source and 95 percent had access to "improved" sanitation. However, these rosy statistics are somewhat misleading. They do not adequately account for periodic water shortages, the generally poor quality of potable water, and increasing contamination of fresh water sources from sewage, agricultural runoff, inadequate disposal of trash, and industrial effluents. Many informal urban areas rely on cesspits and septic tanks as "improved" forms of sanitation. These are often not adequately maintained or disposed of properly, which leads to sewage seeping into the groundwater. In general, rural areas have less access to quality water and sanitation than urban areas, and informal areas are less well served than government-designated urban areas. The informal fringes of even major cities are often not connected to wastewater systems, with the exception of the cities along the Suez Canal.

Most dwellings in Cairo have access to an inside water faucet (96.7 percent in 2008) and the filtered Nile water provided by the public utility meets basic quality criteria for preventing waterborne diseases. Water pressure, however, is often insufficient to many areas and to the upper floors of apartment buildings. Sanitation coverage via sewage connections is high for the urban core and developed neighborhoods, but only about half of Cairo's residents had access to sewage lines in 2008, with everyone else relying on private septic tanks and suction trucks.[25]

Do Egyptians Have Access to Education and Healthcare?

Since the Nasser period, Egypt has rapidly expanded its educational system at all levels. Primary education is now almost universal for both boys and girls. However, the country still suffers from relatively low spending on education. Egypt spends less on education as a share of the total budget than do the nearby countries of Jordan and Tunisia, even though Egypt has a much larger economy and a much larger population. The 2014 constitution mandated increased spending on basic education, but it remains to be seen whether this mandate will be enacted.

The quality of public education remains substandard. Teachers receive low pay and work in decrepit schools with overcrowded classrooms. The curriculum is state-controlled and relies on rote memorization and stressful annual exams rather than critical thinking, research, and discussion skills. Paying for private tutoring in the supposedly public school system is a basic prerequisite for success on exams, which introduces significant income-based inequality into schooling. The use of corporal punishment was long a prominent feature of public schooling. In the UN-Promundo survey, 89 percent of men surveyed remembered being "beaten or physically punished by a teacher" as a child, while 69 percent of the women did.

After primary school, poor families have less access to secondary schooling. Rural poor students are almost as likely to attend primary school as the most wealthy and privileged students. However, only half of disadvantaged boys and less than half of disadvantaged girls are estimated to attend secondary school, whereas wealthy students uniformly attend secondary school.[26] Wealth also determines the quality of instruction that students receive, given the ubiquitous role that private tutoring plays in learning and exam preparation.

As with education, family wealth is an important determinant of whether Egyptians can access decent healthcare. Egypt's healthcare system, like most government services, aspires to universal service and coverage. However, due to underfunding and understaffing, healthcare is substandard for much of the population. The quality of healthcare depends on how much individuals can afford to pay, whether they can access decent facilities and personnel, and whether they have the skills—such as some degree of education—that help them advocate for their family's well-being.

Egypt has a mixed healthcare system with public and private health sectors. The Ministry of Health runs over 4,000 primary care clinics that offer free and low-cost services, but most are inadequately funded and widely viewed as providing poor care. Thus, many families avoid public clinics and seek out university hospitals, medical schools, and private clinics even though these providers are more expensive. Doctors working in the public sector are severely underpaid. They often must work long shifts in public institutions and then hold private evening clinics in order to make ends meet or hold multiple jobs at several public institutions. Prominent government ministries provide healthcare directly to their employees, as part of a system that extends perks through state employment to selected types of employees. These ministries include Defense, Interior, Aviation, Transport, and Electricity.

The government also operates a social insurance system that has gradually expanded to cover more of the population, focused on students, widows, pensioners, veterans, and some poor households. However, only 21 percent of the population had this healthcare coverage in 2008, the latest data available from the World Bank.[27] Even for the insured, the program does not cover many medical costs, meaning that even insured Egyptians must pay approximately three-quarters of all healthcare expenditures out of pocket. The al-Sisi government pledged to create a universal health insurance system by 2030 that would cover care in public and private healthcare facilities, but it is not clear whether or how this expansion will be accomplished.

Egypt's private healthcare sector has expanded significantly since then-president Sadat reopened the Egyptian economy to private economic activity in the 1970s. The facilities range from modern hospitals to mosque clinics run by private voluntary associations to family planning clinics provided by nongovernmental organizations. Most private facilities depend upon user fees, while some also receive charitable contributions and international donor funding.

When the government adequately funds and prioritizes specific healthcare initiatives, its efforts have often improved public health. For example, public health campaigns have successfully combatted the spread of tuberculosis, bilharzia, and diphtheria. As with water and sanitation projects, international donors have played a significant role in supporting targeted healthcare efforts since the 1980s. The US aid agency, USAID, funded successful long-term programs that reduced infant death from diarrheal diseases and improved family planning. Another program focused on increasing immunizations, which lowered the rates of communicable diseases significantly. The vast majority of diseases in Egypt are now non-communicable including cancer, diabetes, cardiovascular diseases, and chronic respiratory illnesses.

Egypt's healthcare system also needs to address health problems arising from inadequate diet and malnutrition, which worsened in the 2000s as global food prices became particularly volatile. The number of children stunted from lack of adequate nutrition rose significantly between 2000 and 2010; UNICEF found that almost a quarter of Egyptian children were stunted, regardless of how well-off their families were.[28] Many Egyptians rely on a diet of subsidized bread, oil, and sugar because of the rising cost of fruits, vegetables, meat, and dairy products. This diet has contributed to escalating rates of obesity, diabetes, and heart disease, which are some of the leading causes of death in Egypt.

Suggested Readings

Nobel Prize-winning economist Amartya Sen is an influential advocate for including rights and capabilities as essential aspects of human development. His books are models of clarity and well worth reading, including *Poverty and Famines: An Essay on Entitlement and Deprivation* (Clarendon, 1981); *Inequality Reexamined* (Harvard, 1992); *Development as Freedom* (Anchor, 1999), and *The Idea of Justice* (Belknap, 2011). The United Nations Development Programme (UNDP) updates the Human Development Indices annually. All its data are freely available online at http://hdr.undp.org/en/content/human-development-index-hdi. UNDP also produces an annual thematic report; the 2016 report is available at http://hdr.undp.org/en/2016-report. The Arab Human Development Reports provide valuable insights into challenges for Egypt and the Arab world and are available online at http://www.arab-hdr.org/. The 2016 report focuses on youth and human development. Household and opinion surveys also shed new light on economic and social issues in Egypt. On gender issues, see S. El Feki, B. Heilman, and G. Barker, eds. *Understanding Masculinities: Results from the International Men and Gender Equality Survey (IMAGES)—Middle East and North Africa*. (UN Women and Promundo-US, 2017). It is available online at: http://promundoglobal.org/wp-content/

uploads/2017/05/IMAGES-MENA-Multi-Country-Report-EN-
16May2017-web.pdf
Essential books analyzing economic development in Egypt and the
Middle East are Melani Cammett, Ishac Diwan, Alan Richards,
and John Waterbury, *A Political Economy of the Middle East*
(Westview, 2015, 4th edition) and Clement Moore Henry and
Robert Springborg, *Globalization and the Politics of Development
in the Middle East* (Cambridge, 2010). The late Samer Soliman's
book, *The Autumn of Dictatorship: Fiscal Crisis and Political Change
under Mubarak* (Stanford, 2011), translated from Arabic, traces
the weakening of the Egyptian state and the services it provides
citizens. Drawing on his decades of experience as an urban planner
in Cairo, David Sims provides a masterful account of how the city
and its residents actually work in *Understanding Cairo: The Logic of
a City Out of Control* (American University in Cairo, 2010). Diane
Singerman brings together a talented group of interdisciplinary
scholars in *Cairo Cosmopolitan: Politics, Culture, and Urban Space in
the New Globalized Middle East* (co-edited with Paul Amar, American
University in Cairo, 2006) and *Cairo Contested: Governance, Urban
Space, and Global Modernity* (Oxford, 2011). Both volumes provide
vivid case studies exploring the contradictory global and local
pressures shaping urban development in Cairo.

5

ENVIRONMENTAL ISSUES, NATURAL RESOURCES, AND QUALITY OF LIFE

How Do Environmental Problems Affect Egypt?

Egypt faces grave environmental problems that negatively impact the health and well-being of its citizens and threaten the country's unique natural and cultural heritages. Like many middle and low-income "developing" countries, Egypt must grapple with environmental problems associated with both poverty and affluence. The environmental harms caused by industrialization, urbanization, and the expansion of consumer societies are costly to address, and the country has both inadequate resources and an unaccountable system of governance to meet these challenges. For example, the most visible environmental problem in many rural and urban areas is trash. Egypt's statistical agency announced in 2017 that approximately 55 percent of the country's households had access to trash disposal through formal or informal garbage collectors, while 45 percent had to get rid of their trash by dumping it in the streets.[1] Mounds of trash in vacant lots, streets, and irrigation canals mar the landscape of both rural and urban Egypt. As in the United States, the volume of trash has expanded from both a growing population and increased consumption of packaging and plastics. Public and private service providers have not kept up with this expansion, particularly in poor and rural areas. Neither the government nor private firms have invested adequately, nor has the government prioritized trash disposal as an important environmental issue.

Egypt's distinctive geography makes its inhabitants particularly vulnerable to environmental problems. The concentration of population and economic activity in the Nile Delta, Nile Valley, and northern coastal regions means that most Egyptians live in close proximity to pollutants generated by industry, transport, and agriculture. Old polluting factories, small workshops, and trucks and vehicles create air pollution, while agricultural runoff, industrial effluents, rising salt concentrations, and solid waste contaminate water supplies and soils. Egypt is further vulnerable to the effects of natural disasters and global climate change—including flooding, earthquakes, and heat waves. Whereas residents in industrialized countries have the benefit of more developed infrastructures and more options for adaptation, many poor Egyptians already suffer from the adverse affects of man-made climate change.

Egypt's densely populated Nile Delta is under threat from several factors. The Delta is slowly subsiding into the sea, as silt from the Nile River that previously replenished the Delta is trapped behind the Aswan High Dam, leading to significant intrusion of salt water into Egypt's fragile coastal aquifers. Man-made global warming is gradually raising sea levels worldwide, a trend that will further salinize Egypt's groundwater supplies. Finally, a massive dam being completed in Ethiopia may diminish the flow of Nile water to the Delta for some years as the dam's reservoir is filled.

Egypt's environmental problems directly affect the health of its citizens, the productivity of its economy, and the viability of its ecosystems. The leading chronic diseases that kill many Egyptians—including cancers, stroke, heart disease, and diseases of the liver and kidneys—have significant yet understudied relationships with toxic wastes, air pollution, and water pollution. Air pollution from sand, dust, and emissions contributes to respiratory infections, asthma, and heart disease in Egypt. A 2016 World Bank study estimated that, in 2013, air pollution contributed to over 39,000 deaths and produced almost a 4 percent reduction in GDP.[2]

Environmental damage also threatens important cultural and natural heritage sites. Egypt relies on revenues from tourism as an important source of foreign exchange to pay for imported food and goods. Yet Egypt has fallen behind many other developing countries in preserving the most important heritage sites and their tourism potential. Air pollution, encroaching urbanization, and salt from rising water tables causes damage not only to the great pyramids and sphinx in Giza but also to many historic Islamic, Christian, and pharaonic sites around the country. The unique coral reefs in the Red Sea, the linchpin of the diving industry in Egypt, are also under threat. Coral bleaching and die-off—a result of rising sea temperatures from global warming combined with dredging, trash dumping, and other sources of pollution—has started to affect these once vibrant, diverse coral colonies. Shredded plastic and solid waste intermittently wash up with various tides and winds in even remote coastal areas. This refuse originates not only in Egypt but also in neighboring countries such as Saudi Arabia and Sudan.

Many of Egypt's severe environmental challenges are shared with other countries in the Middle East and Africa. These include the increasing desertification of land, the negative impacts of man-made climate change, and the widespread loss of biodiversity. The effects of a warming planet are already clearly evident in Egypt and other Arab countries, as they face longer summers and increased periods of intense drought. Drought is punctuated by unusually intense, short periods of rainfall that flood urban areas. Most Arab states must also grapple with limited water and arable land, relatively high population growth rates, hazardous levels of pollution, and generally weak enforcement of environmental laws and regulations.

How Has Egypt Tackled Environmental Issues?

Egypt has gradually expanded state regulation of environmental issues since the 1980s, as have most developing countries. A national environmental agency, designated to coordinate environmental activities between sectoral ministries, was created by presidential decree in 1982, and the country adopted a comprehensive environmental law in 1994. The president also created a minister for environmental affairs, but did not elevate the environmental agency to the status of a ministry. Thus the minister has little power within Egypt's Cabinet and the Egyptian Environmental Affairs Agency has little clout compared with the sectoral ministries devoted to energy, foreign affairs, industry, and tourism. Instead, most of Egypt's environmental improvements have come about through the combined efforts of environmental experts and international donors. Civil society activists have also been important advocates for environmental causes.

Egyptian environmental experts, with financial assistance from the EU, Germany, the United States, Japan, and other donor countries, have made concerted efforts to develop environmental laws and implement pollution control projects. Under Mubarak and now al-Sisi, the Egyptian government compiled lists of environmental projects and asked donors to fund them. These projects include pollution control efforts, energy efficiency measures, the creation of protected areas, and regulations for tourism development. They have led to meaningful improvements. However, their effectiveness has been limited by fragmentation and competition among state authorities, interventions from Egypt's security apparatus, and the political clout of well-connected firms and investors. Enforcement of environmental laws and regulations remains generally weak and is not adequate to address mounting environmental problems. This was particularly apparent after the 2011 revolution and the ensuing withdrawal of police forces around the country. Environmental regulations and laws were routinely flouted, from the hunting of endangered species to the illegal construction of buildings in protected natural areas. Environmental activists have engaged in a variety of tactics to pressure officials for more effective environmental protections. Environmental activism in Egypt takes a range of forms, including spontaneous "wildcat" strikes, sit-ins, petitions of officials, and months-long campaigns organized by networks of activists. Civil society actors have protested garbage crises, the loss of fishing grounds, the importation of coal, the siting of a proposed nuclear power plant, encroachments on national parks and protected areas, and pollution from fertilizer, cement, and chemical plants. Severe restrictions on civil society and rights of expression have limited avenues for protest, yet these types of social mobilization have sometimes been successful. They are most effective when environmental issues clearly lead to ill health and loss of livelihoods, when activists mobilize participants from different classes and organizations, and when environmental campaigns take on a nationalist or populist hue. However, due to government restrictions, broad-based environmental membership organizations as found in the United States and Europe remain rare.

How Water Scarce Is Egypt?

Water holds a particularly prominent place in Egyptian domestic politics and foreign relations, given the country's continued dependence on the Nile River for much of its renewable freshwater supply. The Nile contributes approximately 55.5 billion cubic meters to Egypt's total available water, which was estimated at roughly 74.5 billion cubic meters in 2011–2012. Additional sources of water include 7.5 billion cubic meters of groundwater, 9.2 billion cubic meters of recycled agricultural drainage water, 1.3 billion cubic meters of recycled municipal wastewater, and 50 million cubic meters of desalinated water.[3] Egypt has little prospect of increasing its water share from the

Nile and may face a reduction, as upstream countries such as Ethiopia construct new dams and water diversion projects.

The United Nations and development agencies define national water scarcity as 1,000 cubic meters or less of available water per person. Absolute water scarcity is defined as 500 cubic meters or less per person. In 2013, Egypt was already water scarce, with approximately 762 cubic meters available per person in the country. Without significant new sources of water, the country will reach the threshold for absolute scarcity in a few years. Water scarcity is increasing for several reasons. Most fundamentally, Egypt's share of the Nile flow has stayed the same while population and consumption have rapidly increased.

The government has embarked on a number of initiatives to diversify and conserve water supply. These include expanding water treatment plants to increase the reuse of municipal wastewater and building mixing plants to mix freshwater with agricultural wastewater, thereby diluting pollutants to enable further reuse of water in agriculture downstream. The government also requires all new tourism facilities on the coasts to build their own desalination and treatment plants. In addition, it tries to ensure that new agricultural projects in the desert use drip irrigation and other water-conserving methods. Most new residential areas in satellite cities use treated wastewater for irrigating green spaces. These measures will, however, not be sufficient. In order to better address the problem, the government has tried to raise the funds to build large-scale desalination plants on Egypt's Mediterranean coast. The al-Sisi government also announced that it will try to slow the rate of population growth, in order to reduce the number of people who need water, by prioritizing family planning strategies that had languished in the late Mubarak years.

Safeguarding water quality is just as important as using less water. Polluted water threatens drinking water, human health, the safety of irrigated crops, and industrial production processes requiring clean water. Thus the contamination of water supplies from agricultural, industrial, and municipal discharges is of critical importance. Pollution from trash remains a pressing problem, particularly in areas that lack adequate waste collection and disposal systems. Polluted water has been linked to many illnesses in Egypt, particularly waterborne diseases such as diarrhea and diseases of the liver and kidney.

The Egyptian government, with significant assistance from international donors including the United States, invested in upgrading water treatment plants and sewage treatment plants for major cities over the past several decades. Provision of sanitation in rural areas and poor urban areas is still lagging, however. Given Egypt's growing and urbanizing population, further investment in sewage and wastewater treatment is necessary in order to increase recycling and reuse of water. Wastewater treatment provides a double benefit: it increases the supply of usable water and improves health and welfare of citizens.

Why Is So Much Water Used in Agriculture?

As in most countries, most water consumed in Egypt is used for agriculture. Approximately 86 percent of Egypt's water is used to produce food for people and fodder for animals. Although agriculture accounted for only about 12 percent of Egypt's gross national product in 2016, it provides employment and sustenance to millions of Egyptians. Few families in agricultural areas derive their livelihoods solely from farm income, however; most families seek work in a variety of other economic activities as well as farming.

Farm productivity in the Nile Delta is among the highest in the world, with farmers cultivating various crops with high yields year-round. The country is self-sufficient in several crops, particularly vegetables, fruits, and fodder for livestock. Egypt's extraordinary agricultural productivity is largely a product of the global "green revolution" in the 1970s and

1980s that combined much greater use of chemical fertilizers and pesticides with high-yield seed varieties. These changes also made Egyptian agriculture more pollution-intensive due to nitrate and fertilizer runoff and pesticide contamination of water resources.

For grains, however, Egypt imports 44 percent of its needs. Egypt is the world's largest wheat importer and also a significant importer of rice. These imports of "virtual water" reduce the need for water to grow these crops locally and frees up scarce water for other uses. However, they make the country entirely dependent on holding adequate reserves of US dollars to purchase grains on international markets.

Egypt will face increasingly difficult choices in agriculture as water scarcity deepens. The country cannot afford to build and operate enough large-scale desalination plants to substitute desalinated water for freshwater, as has been done to some extent in Israel and the oil-exporting countries of the Persian Gulf. Many Egyptian farmers still use traditional flood and gravity-fed irrigation systems, particularly in the Nile Delta. These irrigation systems consume far more water than drip and other forms of technologically advanced irrigation, but they are cheap for farmers to use and maintain. Many farmers also claim that flooding the soil flushes out salts and pollutants.

Despite water scarcity, the government remains committed to land reclamation—cultivating trees and crops in the desert—in order to avoid increasing the country's dependence on food imports. However, past experience shows that land reclamation faces serious financial and ecological challenges. The grand plans of successive Egyptian presidents to bring thousands of new hectares under cultivation in the desert have not materialized. Instead, Egyptian farmers have steadily reclaimed arid land near already cultivated areas. They have been successful when they had experience in agriculture, sufficient access to water, and sufficient capital to invest in irrigation and drainage systems. In addition, location matters. When

the reclaimed lands were relatively close to existing transportation networks and urban areas, the prospects for success
were much higher.

As water becomes more scarce, Egypt may need to reallo-
cate more water away from agriculture to cities and higher-
value economic activities. This shift may impose significant
hardship on families dependent on agriculture unless farmers
are provided social safety nets and alternative employment.
In addition, the country will need to ensure that it has sufficient foreign exchange to import more food and goods as the
population grows.

Can Desalination Help Alleviate Water Scarcity?

Like other countries facing freshwater scarcity in the Middle
East, Egypt must invest in desalination plants to convert seawater to usable freshwater. As more groundwater in Egypt's
shallow coastal aquifers becomes contaminated by saltwater
intrusion, some type of desalination will also be needed for
these water sources as well. Saudi Arabia, the other Persian
Gulf states, and Israel rely heavily on desalination to meet their
water needs. The difference between Egypt and these wealthier
countries, however, is that Egypt lacks the financial resources
to pay for these expensive plants. As with other water and
sanitation investments, Egypt will look to the Gulf states and
other international donors to help finance these projects. In
2016, the al-Sisi government announced a US$98.6 million loan
from Kuwait to build five desalination plants on the eastern
coastline of Sinai.

Almost all desalination plants in Egypt, as in the broader
Middle East, rely on electricity generated from fossil fuels.
These fuels generate greenhouse gas emissions and, in Egypt's
case, also represent lost export earnings as the plants consume
oil and natural gas that would otherwise be exported. Using
solar power rather than fossil fuels for desalination plants
would seem an obvious solution. Solar plants can be large or

small scale. Large-scale concentrated solar power plants (CSP) generate thermal electricity by using a large field of mirrors to concentrate solar radiation. In 2016, Morocco announced completion of the first stage of the world's largest concentrated solar plant at Noor-Ouarzazat in the foothills of the Atlas Mountains. It provides an example of an energy option that Egypt might use in the future for desalinization and other purposes.

Why Are Old Egyptian Industries Sources of Serious Pollution?

The industrialization strategy pursued in the 1960s under Nasser focused on building heavy and intermediate industries, including aluminum smelting, fertilizer production, and chemicals. These state-owned industries were supposed to reduce Egypt's reliance on foreign imports. They would be economically viable through the use of subsidized fossil fuels as well as cheap electricity generated by the Aswan Dam. Over time, however, government investment in its state-owned industries stagnated, leaving most of these facilities with outdated systems of production and ineffective pollution controls. This situation was similar to the pollution problems encountered by state-owned industries in the former Soviet Union. These facilities thus became sources of severe industrial pollution, particularly as they were typically located near urban and coastal areas with growing populations.

Egyptian environmental officials and international donors tried to limit pollution from some large state-owned enterprises in the 1980s and 1990s through a variety of measures. The government sold off some industries through privatization programs. Donors supported efforts to upgrade production lines and install new pollution controls at plants producing hazardous emissions or effluents. Several ministers of the environment periodically stepped up efforts to enforce environmental regulations. However, these measures were only partially successful. Private investors were often not interested in purchasing indebted, old state-owned enterprises, while efforts to enforce environmental laws ran up against more powerful ministries such as those controlling industry and petroleum. Most fundamentally, the government did not exert credible pressure on either public or private firms to make needed investments in pollution control and energy efficiency. While there were some successful cases of pollution control, mostly financed by foreign aid, a number of firms remain "hotspots" of pollution.

Pollution is not limited to large enterprises, however. Small- and medium-sized manufacturing enterprises, which make up a small proportion of total industrial production but are extremely numerous, also pose pollution hazards. Their activities are typically unregulated and include food processing, textiles, brick and pottery kilns, chemicals, and metal products. Small and medium-sized firms generally lack access to the credit and expertise that could help them reduce environmental impacts. As with large firms, specific donor-funded projects have helped relocate and upgrade some of their facilities, but these efforts remain the exception rather than the norm.

Why Is Cairo's Air So Polluted?

As one of the fastest growing cities in the world and the largest city in the Middle East, Cairo suffers from severe air pollution. The city is ranked as one of the more polluted cities in the world, overtaken in recent years only by a handful of Chinese and Indian megacities. Poor air quality has had significant health impacts on many residents, making them more likely to develop asthma and other respiratory ailments. It has also led to lost time at work and shorter lifespans. Acute pollution episodes, such as the heat waves that make air quality worse, are particularly dangerous for children and the elderly.

Cairo's air pollution is generated from several sources. These include millions of vehicles clogging its roads in seemingly endless traffic jams, the informal burning of trash in and around the city, industrial emissions from cement and other plants, and the annual burning of fields by farmers to dispose of crop residues. These man-made factors combine with seasonal sand and dust storms, sparse rainfall, and the lack of green spaces to create episodes of severe air pollution. In addition, a thermal inversion traps pollutants over the city for weeks every fall, in what Cairenes refer to as the "black cloud."

Cairo's air quality has improved in some respects since the 1980s. One of the most successful measures to combat urban air pollution was the government's decision to move away from leaded gas in the mid-1990s. Lead additives in gasoline had constituted the most important pathway for lead to enter the environment, leading to high levels of lead exposure for many children in Egypt's cities. Other initiatives to improve air quality include efforts to establish vehicle inspections, convert buses and taxis from diesel to natural gas, and upgrade production processes in some industrial facilities. Efforts to relocate polluting industries to the outskirts of the city have been only partially successful. Many old polluting enterprises—including those owned by the military—remain in the northern and southern reaches of the city.

Inadequate trash collection and burning of trash remain important sources of air pollution in Cairo and throughout Egypt. The nightly burning of garbage—and occasional spontaneous combustion during very hot days—create toxic mixes of fumes. In Cairo, different districts have different garbage collectors, and some providers are far less effective than others. In addition, recycling and composting remain limited. For many years, the Coptic Christian community of the *zabaleen* were the garbage collectors and sorters for the city. However, they have been increasingly excluded from large-scale contracts between the municipality and international waste companies.

Problems of disposing organic waste were made much worse across Egypt in 2009, when the government announced

Photo 5.1 Municipal waste trucks pick up trash in Assiut, Egypt, October 21 2014. Private collectors often carry the waste down from apartments; sort out valuable plastics, paper, and glass; then hand it off to the government collectors. In front and left of the truck is a man carrying government-subsidized *baladi* bread, a staple food for many.

Credit: David Degner

the slaughter of an estimated 300,000 pigs. For much of Egypt's history, pigs consumed some of the country's organic waste. With the global emergence of swine flu, the Mubarak government announced it would cull Egypt's pigs to prevent infection, although the World Health Organization announced that there were no cases of transmission between humans and pigs. The grisly episode epitomized the short-term and arbitrary measures taken by executive decree, without consultation or deliberation with affected communities, which characterize much public policymaking in Egypt.

What Role Do Oil and Natural Gas Play in Egypt's Economy?

Egypt's deposits of oil and natural gas are much less extensive than those of the oil-exporting states of the Persian Gulf, but have nonetheless played a large role in the country's political economy. Oil and natural gas provide 94 percent of Egypt's energy supply, with natural gas alone providing over half of the country's energy. Egypt's oil production peaked in 1993. Since then the government has prioritized developing natural gas for domestic consumption. The strategy of substituting natural gas for oil has allowed remaining oil to be exported for much-needed foreign exchange. Oil exports still accounted for 40 percent of Egypt's total exports in 2016.

Egypt's oil sector was initially developed in the 1930s by large private international firms working in oil fields around the Gulf of Suez. President Nasser nationalized the oil sector in 1962 and established the Egyptian General Petroleum Company, which continued to partner with international oil firms on exploration and development of oil fields. The Egyptian government still receives the export revenue from fossil fuel sales directly since it holds majority ownership in Egypt's oil and gas firms. Egypt, however, always needed the expertise and investment of international energy firms. Even after nationalization, its companies remained in a weak negotiating position for setting contract terms vis-à-vis international energy companies.

The government has subsidized domestic consumption of fossil fuels in order to promote economic development and help poor citizens afford cooking and heating. However, subsidies for oil and gas led investors to focus on industries that used these fuels, since their artificially low prices led to wider profit margins. Particularly after Sadat opened the economy to foreign investment in the mid-1970s, new investors focused on energy-intensive industries such as iron and steel, cement, petrochemicals, and fertilizers. Industrial investment under Mubarak between 2004 and 2010 largely took place in energy-intensive sectors. Because these investments were capital-intensive, they did not generate much employment for ordinary Egyptians. In addition, the government provided significant tax breaks to these large firms. The vast majority of small- and medium-sized enterprises saw no benefit, as their share of manufacturing remained under 10 percent.[4]

Thus, Egypt's reliance on subsidized fossil fuels to attract private investment has had important repercussions for the economy. It skewed credit and governmental support to big energy-intensive projects, jointly owned by foreign investors and the state itself, and contributed to a form of crony capitalism. It also sapped the political will needed to support economic diversification and to expand small- and medium-sized enterprises, which are typically the backbone of innovation and employment in industrializing countries.

Is Egypt's Economy Becoming More or Less Dependent on Fossil Fuels?

Egypt's dependence on fossil fuels is growing. In 2009, the country was the world's eighth largest exporter of liquefied natural gas (LNG). However, by 2016, it was the world's eighth largest importer. How did this happen? The rapid growth of energy-intensive industries during the 2000s created rising demand for energy, particularly as natural gas was used as an input in the production of petrochemicals and fertilizers. The 2008 financial crisis and the 2011 uprising reduced foreign investment in the Egyptian energy sector, dampening domestic production even as consumption rose. By 2012, natural gas supplies were insufficient to keep up with demand, leading to power shortages. Egyptian state-owned energy firms also owed international oil companies a cumulative US$5.2 billion that they were unable to pay in a timely fashion. Foreign firms were thus reluctant to ramp up exploration and production in Egypt.

In 2011/2012, Egypt's ruling generals took several measures that also adversely affected the energy sector. The SCAF shut down the pipeline supplying natural gas to Israel, after armed groups sabotaged it 13 times in the year after the 2011 uprising. In addition, the government limited gas deliveries to

Egypt's two LNG export terminals, both majority owned by multinational consortia, in order to shift the gas to domestic use. These decisions, as well as the inability of Egyptian state-owned firms to pay their debts, led to further declines in foreign investment. In 2013, however, Egypt started to repair its relations with international energy firms by repaying some of the debt it owed and renegotiating repayment schedules.[5]

Egypt's energy picture has begun to change with dramatic new finds of offshore natural gas. The discovery of large gas fields off Egypt's Mediterranean coast is likely to make the country self-sufficient in natural gas in a few years and has led international firms to resume investment. One new field is estimated to hold 30 trillion cubic feet of gas, making it the largest natural gas field in the Mediterranean. The energy sector attracted US$28 billion in foreign investment in 2015, which emboldened the Egyptian government to announce that energy firms could resume exporting natural gas in 2020.

The question that Egyptian policymakers face, however, is whether to repeat the choices of previous decades by subsidizing oil and gas prices. Egypt must offer competitive terms to international energy companies in order to attract their investment capital and technological skills. However, Egypt's high subsidies in the 2000s skewed domestic industrial investment toward large-scale projects in energy-intensive sectors, which benefited from cheap fuel. These competing pressures have led to inconsistent government policies. The al-Sisi government reduced subsidies in 2014, then reversed direction in 2015 by increasing subsidies for oil and gas supplied to industries, and then cut fuel subsidies again in 2016 under an agreement with the International Monetary Fund.

Regardless of natural gas abundance, energy specialists have encouraged the government to adopt several policy changes. In their view, the government should improve regulatory and financial incentives to encourage energy conservation. It should also diversify its energy mix. The government has approved construction of the country's first nuclear plant,

overriding protests by local communities, but a more promising direction is renewable energies given Egypt's ample sun
and wind resources. Several successful large-scale wind farms
were built in the 2000s along the Gulf of Suez.

Some planners have also proposed the construction of large-
scale solar arrays in Egypt and other parts of North Africa that
would produce electricity for domestic use and for export
to Europe. The most well known of these projects, Desertec,
envisions an integrated European–North African electricity
grid based on the export of solar-produced power from North
Africa to Europe. Tunisia and Morocco have already signed
contracts to build concentrated solar plants as part of this project. Jordan has also announced several solar plants under development. A southern Mediterranean regional power grid
already exists, which enabled Egypt to export electricity to
Jordan and Libya in the past, and there are plans to connect
Tunisia to the grid. If sufficient outside investment can be
mobilized, exports of solar power could generate income—and
foreign exchange—for the Egyptian government. However,
the plans for the export of solar power rely on political stability
across North Africa, the mobilization of significant investment
from global banks and investors, and the ability of Europe to
further integrate its own electrical grids. While these ambitious plans are unfolding, Egypt could expand smaller-scale
decentralized solar systems. However, little governmental effort has been exerted toward distributing or subsidizing small-
scale solar technologies. This is an area where ample room
exists for low-cost environmental improvement.

How Vulnerable Is Egypt to Man-Made Climate Change?

Man-made climate change already threatens the health and
livelihood of many Egyptians. Rising temperatures, severe
flashfloods, less and more variable rainfall, and intensified
droughts are well-documented in Egypt, as across much of the
Middle East and North Africa. Heat waves in the summer are

amplified by the heat island effect of cities and the lack of access to air conditioning. As with the ill effects of air pollution, children and the elderly are most vulnerable to extreme heat. In agriculture, southern parts of Egypt already face high temperatures that are at the limit of what many crops can tolerate.

Egypt's location and limited resources make the country particularly vulnerable to the effects of man-made climate change. As the ice stored in polar regions and mountain glaciers melts more rapidly than predicted, scientists are revising upward their estimates of global sea-level rise. Any rise in sea level due to climate change will have grave impacts on the Nile Delta as it will force large numbers of people to move, and seawater will infiltrate shallow freshwater aquifers. Sea-level rise will also have adverse impacts on a range of economic activities located in coastal areas that sustain many Egyptians.

Like other developing countries, Egypt bears little historical responsibility for global warming even as its population is more vulnerable to the impacts than those living in developed countries. Since Egypt industrialized relatively late, and much of the population is poor and consumes little fossil fuels, Egypt emits relatively few greenhouse gases per person in comparison with more advanced industrial countries. For example, dividing Egypt's total carbon dioxide emissions in 2015 by its population yields 2.5 tons of carbon dioxide emitted for each person. The United States, by way of comparison, emitted 16.1 tons of carbon dioxide per person in 2015. Egypt's total emissions for 2015 are less than 1 percent of the global total (.68 percent), while the United States accounted for over 14 percent of global CO_2 emissions.

Egypt was a signatory to the Kyoto Protocol and joined the Paris Climate Agreement. The country complied with its Kyoto mandates by conducting national inventories of greenhouse gas emissions and identifying mitigation measures. Egyptian engineers also utilized the financing available under Kyoto's Clean Development Mechanism to undertake over one hundred projects. These included switching from heavy, low quality

fuel oils to natural gas, and undertaking energy-efficient infrastructure projects in the industrial, water, and electrical sectors.
Egyptian environmental scientists have also emphasized
the importance of embarking on proactive adaptation measures for coastal areas, poor households, and the agricultural
sector. However, they face an uphill battle. The government
is focused on stabilizing the economy and crushing dissent.
The communities most vulnerable to climate change include
fishermen, small farmers, and herders, and they have little political clout. Similarly, poor residents in informal areas, who have
less access to protective infrastructure and less income to spend
on water and air conditioning, are also more likely to suffer from
flash floods, heat waves, and other extreme weather events.

Egypt's public and private sectors will increasingly need to
include the costs of climate change adaptation in their investment decisions. In addition, the government will need to steadily
increase the funds it allocates for facing this challenge. The Paris
Climate Accord and other agreements have increased the funds
available from international donors, but they are nowhere near
sufficient to cover the anticipated damages to countries such as
Egypt. Worse, as in other development efforts, some programs
benefit international consultants and development firms more
than affected communities.

Although the Trump administration withdrew the United
States from the Paris Climate Accords in 2017, mitigation
efforts by leading world economies must be ramped up to
avoid even greater harm to countries such as Egypt. Climate
change in Egypt amplifies existing environmental problems of
desertification, scarce water, and polluted ecosystems that already negatively affect many Egyptians.

Suggested Readings

Two excellent edited volumes that introduce readers to the fascinating
environmental histories of Egypt and the Middle East are
Environmental Imaginaries of the Middle East and North Africa, edited

by Diana Davis and Edmund Burke III (Ohio University, 2012) and *Water on Sand: Environmental Histories of the Middle East and North Africa*, edited by Alan Mikhail (Oxford, 2013). For an analysis of modern environmental issues in Egypt and efforts to address them, see Jeannie Sowers, *Environmental Politics in Egypt: Activists, Experts, and the State* (Routledge, 2013). Jessica Barnes provides a compelling ethnographic account of how Egyptian farmers cope with water scarcity and other agricultural challenges in *Cultivating the Nile: The Everyday Politics of Water in Egypt* (Duke, 2014). For insights into how Arab governments have approached the challenges of climate change, see John Waterbury, "The Political Economy of Climate Change in the Arab Region," United Nations Development Program, Research Paper Series, 2013, https://pdfs. semanticscholar.org/88b7/1312fee4471c7bdcde08e8338be2ab50 5ae8.pdf. For Egypt specifically, see Jeannie Sowers, "Resources and Revenues: The Political Economy of Climate Initiatives in Egypt" in Charles Roger and David Held, eds, *Climate Change Governance in the Developing World* (Polity, 2013).

6

RELIGION

What Role Do Coptic Christians Play in Egyptian Politics and Society?

Egypt held an important position in the early development of Christianity. In the three centuries after the death of Jesus, Alexandria was one of the primary centers for debate over the doctrine and beliefs of the new faith. The practice of Christian monasticism emerged in Egypt, and some of the earliest monasteries in Christendom were established in Upper Egypt.

In the fifth century, several bishops of Alexandria put forward doctrinal positions regarding the nature of Christ that differed sharply from those of theologians in Rome and Constantinople. The dispute centered on whether Christ was a human who became divine (the Egyptian position) or whether he was inherently divine. The ambitions of religious leaders in Alexandria, Rome, and Constantinople also played a role in the debate, as they jockeyed for influence in the Christian world. The Egyptian bishops invoked this doctrinal disagreement as the basis for creating a separate church, the Egyptian Coptic Church, and selected their own pope. The Coptic community in Egypt also developed a distinctive language rooted in the language of the ancient Egyptians.

By the sixth century, the large majority of Egyptians were Christian. The spread of Islam to Egypt in the seventh century led to the conversion of many Copts. Others migrated over the ensuing centuries to destinations throughout the world. By the early twenty-first century, Coptic Christians constituted roughly 8–10 percent of Egypt's population and were the largest Christian community in the Middle East.

Copts have played a prominent role in modern Egyptian history. For example, during the years after World War I, Copts held senior positions in the Wafd party and in the Wafd governments that led the charge for Egyptian independence. In 1928, a Copt (Wissa Wassef) was elected speaker of the Parliament. However, the prominence of Copts in political life began to recede under Nasser and declined even more sharply under Sadat. Sadat emphasized Egypt's Islamic identity in an effort to build a stronger base of support for his rule and to offset the influence of leftists in the country's politics and society. He added clauses to the Constitution specifying that Islam was the religion of the state and that Sharia was the primary source of law. He also allowed Islamist groups such as the Muslim Brotherhood to organize more widely on university campuses and in society. Each of these steps redefined Egyptian identity in a manner less inclusive of the Coptic community.

Mubarak continued this policy and also altered the structure through which Copts interacted with the state. Prior to the 1980s, Copts, like other Egyptian citizens, participated in civil society groups and political parties and utilized the law to protect their interests. While these avenues remained open, Mubarak also cultivated the Coptic pope as the official representative of the Coptic community to the state in an effort to consolidate support for his regime. Copts were encouraged to convey their concerns through the Coptic clerical hierarchy rather than through secular organizations or political parties. This change expanded the social and political power of the Coptic pope. However, it also meant that Copts were increasingly compartmentalized as a community. There were fewer arenas where Copts regularly interacted with Muslims, and the two communities began to function separately from each other.

These changes coincided with the strengthening of Salafi Islam. The Salafis espouse a very literal and narrow conception of Islam that is deeply critical of Christians and views them with suspicion, claiming that they are a fifth column acting on behalf of Christian powers. While the large majority of Egyptian Muslims do not share this view, it has become part of Egyptian cultural life and influences the debate about Copts and their place in Egyptian society.

The increasing isolation of Copts was manifest in several ways. They were excluded from senior posts within the bureaucracy and the security apparatus. Some Copts were prosecuted under Egypt's blasphemy laws for comments deemed disrespectful toward Islam. The regime also enforced a long-standing law that restricted the construction and renovation of churches, making it almost impossible for Copts to build or renovate churches. In addition, sporadic sectarian attacks on Christians increased in the 1990s and 2000s, particularly in Upper Egypt. Copts found that the perpetrators often were not prosecuted by Egyptian courts and, in some cases, the local police failed to intervene to protect Copts from attacks.

The Coptic clerical leadership concluded that the best way to protect their community was to cultivate a close relationship with the regime. During the Mubarak era, the Coptic pope met regularly with the president. During the January 2011 uprising against Mubarak, the church called on Copts to refrain from joining the demonstrations. Nonetheless, many Copts participated in the hope that a truly democratic regime would restore their full equality as citizens. A prominent Coptic businessman, Naguib Sawiris, started and funded a political party (the Free Egyptians), and several Christian intellectuals helped to found the Social Democratic Party.

However, Copts' hopes that the 2011 uprising would inaugurate a new era for their community faded quickly. Sporadic attacks on Coptic churches continued in the months after Mubarak's removal. In October 2011, a group of Copts and Muslims demonstrated together in front of the national television building in the Maspero neighborhood to protest the government's failure to adequately respond to these attacks. The military government (the SCAF) dispersed the protest with remarkable brutality, killing at least 24 unarmed demonstrators. The incident became known as the "Maspero Massacre" and has been invoked on several occasions as evidence that the security apparatus not only fails to protect Christians but sometimes suppresses them.

Nonetheless, the Coptic leadership believed that the military was more likely to protect their community than any other actor in Egyptian society. They were particularly concerned about the electoral successes of the Muslim Brotherhood, which they feared would lead to further isolation of their community. When the military announced its decision to remove the Brotherhood's Muhammad Mursi from power in July 2013, the Coptic pope appeared on the stage with then-defense minister al-Sisi and expressed his support for the military's action. The pope encouraged al-Sisi to run for president and called on Copts to approve the new Constitution that his government drafted.

Islamist opponents of al-Sisi turned some of their wrath on Copts and launched a new wave of violence against Coptic churches and businesses in the months following Mursi's removal. The rise of a radical Islamic group in Sinai, Ansar Beit al-Maqdis, led to additional attacks. After this group proclaimed its allegiance to Islamic State (IS) in 2014, it issued several statements proclaiming that it would target Egypt's Christian population. Copts soon faced a brutal wave of violence that included attacks on Coptic churches during Christmas and Easter that killed hundreds of worshippers.

Al-Sisi has stated his strong commitment to protecting Copts and affirmed that they are full and equal citizens of Egypt. However, he has not yet adequately addressed many of their grievances—particularly, discrimination against them in the workplace and continuing restrictions on the construction and renovation of churches. In addition, al-Sisi may be reluctant to advocate for Copts aggressively out of fear that such a step would provoke a response from radical Islamists that would worsen the problem. The Coptic community remains caught in an increasingly deteriorating situation—targeted by brutal radical groups with a state unable or unwilling to protect them. In the face of these conditions, many Copts have chosen to emigrate.

What Is Establishment Islam? What Are Its Primary Institutions?

In Islamic political thought, the state is an important actor. It helps to create an Islamic community by enforcing laws that comply with Islamic principles. It also educates the community in the doctrine and practices of the faith and facilitates the performance of key Islamic duties, such as charitable giving.

These principles have been applied in a variety of ways throughout Egyptian history and have led to the emergence of several state institutions that influence Islam's role in public and private life.

The Ministry of Religious Endowments (Awqaf) manages several thousand endowments of land and other assets given in the past to support charitable causes. The ministry also oversees Egypt's state-run mosques. The ministry maintains the mosques, grants licenses for new mosques, certifies preachers, and monitors sermons. The state first began to manage religious endowments in the early nineteenth century. In the 1960s, Nasser nationalized all of the country's religious endowments, which dramatically expanded the ministry's resources and influence.

Dar al-Ifta issues official but non-binding interpretations of Islamic law (fatwas) on matters related to state policy. Its rulings have addressed issues such as the privatization of public companies, reform of divorce laws, and the peace treaty with Israel. It was founded in the late nineteenth century by the country's ruler (the Khedive) and charged with issuing fatwas that would adapt the faith to modern conditions and reinforce the modernization projects undertaken by the government.

Al-Azhar Mosque and University was founded in the tenth century and is the oldest and most respected institution of Islamic learning in the Sunni Muslim world. Al-Azhar runs a network of primary and secondary religious schools throughout the country with over 1 million students. Al-Azhar University has over 90,000 students from all over the world and an extensive faculty that trains the country's preachers and religious scholars. In the early 1960s, its curriculum was expanded to include secular subjects such as biology, physics, literature, and economics.

Al-Azhar is also home to the Council of Senior Religious Scholars, which serves as the country's authoritative voice on matters of Islamic doctrine. This council has the power to review all forms of media in Egypt and censor content that it considers contrary to Islamic principles. The council also selects the Sheikh of al-Azhar and nominates the leader of the Dar al-Ifta (the Mufti). In addition, it issues non-binding fatwas on an enormous range of topics, including state policy. In this regard, it competes with the Dar al-Ifta. However, the Dar al-Ifta is generally considered the government's religious lawyer, who produces rulings that align with the government's wishes. Al-Azhar, in contrast, is considered a more independent body whose rulings carry greater scholarly credibility and authority.

The leaders of Egypt's political system are acutely aware of al-Azhar's stature and have tried to gain its support. For example, when Egypt's military removed Muhammad Mursi from power in July 2013, the news was conveyed to the public in a televised speech by then-defense minister al-Sisi with the Sheikh of al-Azhar sitting in the background, which signaled that the military's action had al-Azhar's backing. Al-Azhar also cooperated in the subsequent crackdown against the Muslim Brotherhood by dismissing Brotherhood appointees from positions within the University and expelling Azhari students who expressed support for the Brotherhood. In addition, the al-Sisi regime has attempted to enlist al-Azhar in the confrontation with radical Islamists by calling on its sheiks to develop and preach a moderate conception of the faith that will refute the views of the radicals.

While the leaders of al-Azhar have expressed their willingness to play this role, the vastness of the religious bureaucracy makes such an effort difficult to implement. Indeed, the religious bureaucracy is so byzantine that different parts of it are sometimes at odds. For example, in 2016 the Ministry of Religious Endowments issued a directive requiring that all preachers throughout the country present the same sermon during the Friday prayers, which would be written by the ministry. Al-Azhar's leaders indicated that they opposed this idea and, if it were to unfold, the sermons should be written by their scholars rather than by the ministry's bureaucrats. After a surprisingly public spat that lasted several months, al-Azhar prevailed, but not without significant objections from the ministry.

The size and complexity of the religious bureaucracy pose a continuing challenge for Egypt's leaders. Ideally, they would like to use these religious institutions to enhance their legitimacy and endorse their policies. However, if government officials attempt to manage them directly, they will appear to the public as merely appendages of the regime and lose their religious credibility—and, thus, much of their effectiveness. On the other hand, if the regime grants them too much autonomy, they could become centers of opposition or become so hopelessly divided that they are incapable of carrying out their duties. Egypt's leaders continue to seek a balance that allows them enough control to facilitate some of their goals without holding these institutions so tightly that the embrace discredits them.

When and Why Did the Muslim Brotherhood Emerge?

The Muslim Brotherhood was founded in 1928 by Hasan al-Banna, a schoolteacher in the Suez Canal city of Ismailia. This city was home to most of the British soldiers who patrolled the Canal zone. As a consequence, al-Banna encountered British soldiers on a daily basis and his views were, in part, a product of his resentment over the power and influence of these non-Muslim foreigners.

Al-Banna borrowed some of the ideas put forward by earlier Islamic reformers mentioned in Chapter 2. In his view, Egyptians had wandered from the spiritual and moral precepts of Islam. As a consequence, the country had become poor, divided, and corrupt. Britain exploited these weaknesses to maintain a painful and humiliating occupation. The only hope for rebuilding the nation's pride and power lay in a return to Islam and, particularly, the implementation of Sharia (Islamic jurisprudence). Al-Banna wrote that without the Sharia, Muslims were "a people without direction." With it, they acquired a sense of strength and purpose "deeply rooted in our history, our society, and our circumstances."[1] Furthermore, he argued that the implementation of Sharia should reflect the wishes and interests of the Islamic community. Sharia was not an ossified set of codes from the seventh century. Rather, it was an attempt by devout Muslims to apply the moral precepts of the Quran and the Sunnah (the sayings and actions of the Prophet) to the challenges of daily life. As these challenges changed, Sharia should change while still pursuing the constant goal of creating a more devout Islamic community.

The Brotherhood was initially vague about its political objectives. The organization was centered on the charismatic personality of al-Banna and a small group of followers who dutifully implemented his instructions. The details of the organization's objectives emerged gradually through the sermons and letters of al-Banna. In 1945, these were codified into a set of bylaws. They state that the Brotherhood will pursue five goals: precise explanation of the Quran based on its original meaning while accommodating "the spirit of the age"; unification of Egypt and the Islamic world based on the principles of the Quran; strengthening Egyptian society by increasing national wealth, reducing inequality, and providing social services; liberating all Arab countries of any foreign presence; and pursuing world cooperation and peace based on freedom, human rights, and Islam.[2] Al-Banna elaborated several other goals for the organization through additional statements, letters, and sermons. He called for banning all political parties, on the grounds that they aggravated social and class divisions within society. He supported ending corruption in government, strengthening the independence of the judiciary, and expanding the government's role in supervising education and public morality.[3]

Al-Banna further argued that Egypt suffered from two forms of imperialism. The first was the obvious, external variety at the hands of Britain, which entailed a large British troop presence and extensive British influence over Egyptian politics and policy. The second was a more insidious "internal colonialism" carried out by local elites who shared Britain's goals and benefited from its presence. In order to achieve true independence, Egyptians must defeat both of these forms of imperialism. This view led the Brotherhood to undertake violent attacks against both the British colonial forces and their Egyptian allies.

Under al-Banna's leadership, the Brotherhood developed two factions. The "secret apparatus," led by Ahmad Sanadi, favored armed confrontation with the regime. In the late 1940s, this militant wing was held responsible for the assassination of a judge and a prime minister, the bombing of several government buildings, and a plot to overthrow the government. Al-Banna denied that the Brotherhood was behind the attacks. Nonetheless, he was assassinated in 1949, probably by members of the secret police seeking revenge for the murder of the prime minister.

The more widely known and popular faction, led by Hasan al-Hudeibi, called for education and preaching that would develop the spiritual awareness of the Egyptian people and gradually build public support for implementing Sharia. During his lifetime, al-Banna was largely able to avoid an overt clash between these two factions because of his personal charisma and his credibility as founder of the movement. His death led to a protracted internal battle between them. Al-Hudeibi eventually assumed the post of General Guide, but he never gained the obedience of the more violent Sanadi faction. These two different strands of the Brotherhood's ideology—one endorsing peaceful participation in society and politics, the other favoring violent confrontation—continue to shape the organization's strategy and operations to the present day.

Al-Banna's successors in the leadership of the Brotherhood briefly attempted to cooperate with the Nasser regime when it came to power in 1952. However, the Brotherhood ran sharply afoul of Nasser in October 1954 when a militant member of the organization attempted to assassinate him. Nasser responded with a comprehensive crackdown that pushed the Brotherhood underground for the remainder of his regime. Some members of the Brotherhood who suffered this repression turned to the confrontational tactics of the Sanadi faction.

In particular, a Brotherhood thinker imprisoned under Nasser—Sayyid Qutb—argued that the brutality and corruption of Egypt's government was so extreme that it defied even the most basic precepts of Islam and, as a consequence, the country was in a state of pre-Islamic ignorance (*jahiliyya*). He concluded that devout Muslims had an obligation to forcibly overthrow the regime. Any tolerance of it, or cooperation with it, was sinful and hopeless. Nasser confronted this threat of rebellion quickly and aggressively. He executed Qutb and several of his disciples in 1965 and arrested over 18,000 Brotherhood members who were suspected of sympathizing with Qutb's views. Nonetheless, Qutb's ideas continued to find some supporters. His writings also provided the ideological foundation for several subsequent Islamic radical groups such as al-Qaeda and Islamic State.

The Brotherhood re-emerged in the mid-1970s under Nasser's successor, Anwar Sadat. He calculated that a limited return of the Brotherhood to public life would offset the influence of leftists, particularly on university campuses. Hosni Mubarak adopted a similar approach and allowed the Brotherhood to organize in universities and professional syndicates and to publish its views in newspapers and magazines. The Brotherhood also created an extensive social service network that provided housing, education, food, and medical care to the poor and lower middle class. It was not permitted to form a political party due to an Egyptian law that bans parties based on religion. However, the Brotherhood was allowed to participate in electoral alliances with established parties, which enabled it to win a few seats in Parliament in the 1980s and 1990s.

The opportunities for electoral competition improved in 2005, when Mubarak—under American pressure—agreed to allow a relatively open parliamentary election. Although he eventually retreated from this promise as the balloting unfolded, he permitted the campaigning phase of the election to occur with remarkably little interference. The Brotherhood was able to compete openly using its own name and to support a group of independent candidates. Its campaign platform called for legal and institutional constraints on state power, protection of many civil and political rights, the rule of law, and the principle that laws should be written by elected representatives who are accountable to the people.

After the January 2011 uprising, the Brotherhood had the opportunity to create its own political party—the Freedom and Justice Party. Its platform reiterated the organization's earlier campaign documents and called for the creation of a competitive democracy that protected civil and political rights. In the parliamentary elections of 2011/2012, it won 42 percent of the seats in the lower house of parliament and 58 percent of the contested seats in the upper house. In the presidential election in June 2012, the Brotherhood's candidate—Muhammad Mursi—won with 52 percent of the vote. As discussed in Chapter 1, the Brotherhood's term in power was brief and turbulent. In July 2013, the military removed Mursi from office and then declared the Brotherhood a terrorist organization.

Who Are the Salafis? What Is Their Role in Egyptian Politics?

Salafis in Egypt advocate unwavering adherence to a literal reading of the core texts of Islam, the Quran and the Sunnah. In their view, the Prophet and the five generations that succeeded him practiced the faith in its purest form. Indeed, their name is a reference to the earliest generations of Muslims (*salaf* means "ancestors"). In their view, the cultural and doctrinal diversity that emerged within Islam as it became a world religion corrupted this early practice. Their goal is to return the practice of Islam to its original form and expunge the accretions and innovations that supposedly distorted the faith over the past 1,300 years. Their view of the faith includes conservative social practices such as prohibiting men and women from mixing and avoiding contact with non-Muslims. Egyptian Salafis have been influenced by religious thinking and practices in Saudi Arabia and have benefited from financial support from associations and individuals in the Arab Gulf countries. In addition, Salafi ideas and practices from the Gulf have been conveyed to Egypt by the millions of Egyptians who worked in the Gulf over the past 40 years and then returned home.

Egypt's Salafis aim to transform society from below through preaching, education, and social services. Their leaders emphasize the importance of accepting the existing political regime, even if it is repressive, and to not risk the instability that could flow from an attempt at political change. For most of their history, Salafi groups opposed participation in politics on the grounds that the compromises required by political life would corrupt and weaken their followers. They were also critical of democracy which, in their view, pitted believers against one another and therefore fueled division within the Muslim community. They further feared that the democratic process would produce laws that were incompatible with their strict interpretation of Islamic doctrine.

Salafis have proven very adept at harnessing modern technology to their cause. They have made particularly skillful use of satellite television, which became widespread in Egypt in the 1990s. They established several satellite TV channels filled with programs featuring speeches and commentaries by Salafi sheiks. These programs found a large audience, in part because many Egyptians had grown disillusioned with al-Azhar University and other institutions of establishment Islam that had fallen under the control of the state. By the early 2000s, Salafi broadcasts were among the most widely watched programs in Egypt.

In addition, Salafis developed an extensive social service network that provided medical care, education, and food. As the country's fiscal crisis deepened, the state lacked the capacity to meet the basic needs of many of its citizens. Salafi groups moved into this vacuum and met these needs, while also spreading their religious views to those whom they served.

The Salafis present themselves as an alternative to the Muslim Brotherhood. For most of the past 45 years, the Brotherhood called on its followers to engage in political life and participate in professional syndicates, student unions at universities, and national elections. The Salafis, in contrast, instructed their followers to avoid politics and focus on their personal spirituality and on spreading their message as widely as possible. The regime allowed their influence to grow because it saw them as a religious and social movement that posed no challenge to the political order. It also hoped that the Salafis would draw supporters away from the Brotherhood, whose political ambitions were of great concern to Egypt's rulers. When the large protests of January 2011 began, the leaders of the Salafi movement initially criticized the protesters and called on their followers to stay home. Only after 15 days of demonstrations, when it became likely that Mubarak would exit from power, did the Salafis support the uprising and the removal of Mubarak.

After Mubarak stepped down, the Salafis developed a taste for politics. They established several political parties, the largest of which was the al-Nur (light) party. The decision to enter politics ran counter to decades of Salafi doctrine. Al-Nur's leaders justified this shift by emphasizing the need to expand the role of Islam in Egyptian society during this period of transition. They also wanted to counteract what they regarded as the excessive influence of liberal ideas over the political and constitutional debates that erupted in the wake of Mubarak's departure.

The al-Nur party set its focus tightly on discussions of a new Constitution. In order to maximize its influence in these discussions, the party's leaders began building alliances with a variety of groups, which necessitated adopting positions at odds with previous Salafi teachings. For example, the al-Nur party's campaign platform stated that the party supported democracy within the framework of Sharia. It backed many civil and political rights, including freedom of assembly, speech, inquiry, and property ownership; "equal dignity" for men and women, with women permitted to undertake higher education, pursue careers outside the home, and vote; full legal equality for Copts, who would be permitted to utilize their religious laws in matters of personal status; and a Parliament chosen through free elections and possessing full powers to draft legislation. The ideological flexibility shown by al-Nur provoked great controversy within the movement. Supporters of this approach argued that it was necessary in order to serve the best interests of the Salafi movement and the Islamic community. Critics argued that it entailed precisely the compromising of doctrinal principles that led Salafis to avoid politics for most of their history.

The al-Nur party received a surprisingly strong endorsement in the 2011/2012 parliamentary elections, winning

21 percent of the seats in the lower house and 25 percent in the upper making it the second-largest party in both houses, after the Brotherhood's Freedom and Justice Party. Its success was attributed, in part, to its many decades of providing social services to poor Egyptians who then cast their ballots for the party.

After the Brotherhood won control of both the Parliament and the presidency in 2012, Salafi leaders became concerned that their rival would begin to dominate the religious and political arena and advance a conception of the faith that lacked the purity and authenticity of the Salafi vision. Salafis became particularly worried as the Brotherhood appointed its supporters to the key state institutions that supervise the practice of Islam, including the Ministry of Religious Endowments. Thus, when the military intervened in July 2013 to remove Muhammad Mursi from the presidency, the al-Nur party and other Salafi groups supported the coup. They also supported al-Sisi's election as president.

They hoped that the removal of the Brotherhood would create an opportunity for Salafi groups to expand their influence. However, they were soon disappointed. The government increased the state's control over the country's mosques, including the mosques where Salafi sheiks preach to their followers. The leaders of mosques are now required to pass a written proficiency test on Islamic principles. If they fail, they are not permitted to preach. This is a point of considerable concern to Salafis, who often lack formal religious training. The state also monitors the budgets and programs of mosques far more closely and insists that their activities conform to government policies. These steps have limited the Salafis' capacity to recruit new members and sustain their existing networks.

What Is Ansar Beit Al-Maqdis (Sinai Province)?

The largest group in Egypt that espouses violence to change the existing order is Ansar Beit al-Maqdis (Supporters of

Jerusalem) (ABM). The organization emerged in the northern portion of the Sinai Peninsula in the 2000s. The roots of its support lie largely in the central government's neglect of this region. As noted in Chapter 4, the quality of state services such as education, medical care, and infrastructure is much poorer in Sinai than in the more heavily populated Nile Valley. The local Bedouin also face discrimination in employment and housing, which further deepens their sense of persecution at the hands of a distant elite in Cairo.

ABM carried out its first attack in 2010, when it bombed the pipeline that exports natural gas to Israel. It conducted another 13 attacks on this pipeline during 2011 and early 2012. In ABM's view, the Egyptian regime was taking gas from Sinai and sending it to Egypt's adversary while denying the people of Sinai basic public services and decent employment. ABM also began carrying out attacks against Israel, which included launching rockets against the Israeli port city of Eilat. The organization released a video in 2011 that reiterated its rejection of the peace treaty with Israel and its opposition to the nascent democracy emerging in post-Mubarak Egypt. It presented a view similar to some Salafis—that democracy places sovereignty in the hands of the people, rather than God; and that democratic practices could produce legislation that is at odds with a literal interpretation of the Quran.

The removal of Muhammad Mursi from office in July 2013 sparked an intensification of ABM's attacks, which accelerated further after the regime began a broad campaign of repression against Islamists. ABM began conducting attacks outside of Sinai, including an attempt to assassinate the Minister of Interior in September 2013. The group attacked a military intelligence building near the Suez Canal in October 2013 as well as police stations in Cairo and in areas north of the capital. ABM further declared that the army and the police had abandoned Islam and, thus, were legitimate targets wherever they could be found. By one count, ABM has killed over 1,000 Egyptian soldiers since the start of its insurgency.[4]

As the Egyptian army responded to the ABM threat, it used increasingly aggressive tactics that entailed destroying houses and neighborhoods and inflicting significant civilian casualties. For example, in an effort to stem the flow of weapons and fighters from Gaza into Sinai, the Egyptian military destroyed all houses and businesses along a five-kilometer stretch of the border. The army provided the local population with only minimal compensation. These tactics have further aggravated the grievances that lead young people to join ABM. The Egyptian military's response to ABM has also included extensive coordination with Israel's security forces, which monitor the Sinai closely and occasionally carry out raids. ABM's leaders have cited this cooperation as evidence of the regime's abandonment of Islam and, thus, further justification for violence against all representatives of the state.

After an attack in October 2014 that killed 33 security personnel, ABM pledged its allegiance to Islamic State and changed its name to Sinai Province (*Wilayet Sinai*). It adopted IS tactics such as beheadings, particularly of alleged collaborators, and undertook bolder and more sophisticated attacks. For example, in January 2015 its fighters killed more than 40 people in simultaneous attacks on five targets including a military base, a police club, and a military hotel. In July 2015, it released photos of an attack with a guided antitank missile on a Navy vessel off the northern coast of Sinai. The group took responsibility in November 2015 for downing an airliner filled with Russian tourists returning home after vacationing in Sinai, killing 224 people and striking a devastating blow to Egypt's tourism industry.

The organization's leaders seek to create a society similar to what IS attempted to build in eastern Syria. It includes a "morals police" to enforce strict rules against smoking, men shaving their beards, or women exposing their faces. ABM/Sinai Province has destroyed tombs and shrines in the areas that it controls, on the grounds that these monuments are un-Islamic, and has confiscated satellite dishes and shut down video stores to halt the spread of cultural values that it considers at odds with Islam.

One of the most deeply troubling developments with ABM/Sinai Province is its decision to target Egypt's Christian community in an effort to aggravate sectarian tensions and, thereby, destabilize the country. The group took responsibility for bombing Coptic churches in December 2014 and December 2016. It also claimed responsibility for bombing two churches on Palm Sunday in 2017, leaving at least 44 dead and many injured. It has called for attacks on Christians throughout Egypt, sparking a wave of smaller assaults on Coptic churches and businesses.

Many analysts note that a key component of the fight against ABM/Sinai Province lies in addressing the poverty and lack of economic opportunity in Sinai. Toward this end, the government has announced a US$1 billion plan to develop Sinai through investments in housing, infrastructure, agriculture, and light industry. In addition, many observers emphasize the need for the government to change its tactics to minimize civilian casualties, avoid collective punishment of Bedouin tribes, and reduce damage to civilian homes and property.

Suggested Readings

For an insightful discussion of the challenges currently facing Copts, written by an accomplished Coptic journalist, see Mariz Tadros, *Copts at the Crossroads* (American University in Cairo, 2013).
For academic treatments of the same topic, try Laure Guirguis, *Copts and the Security State* (Stanford, 2017) or Elizabeth Iskander, *Sectarian Conflict in Egypt* (Routledge, 2012). For a concise overview of establishment Islam in Egypt, see Nathan J. Brown's short essay, "Official Islam in the Arab World," Carnegie Endowment for International Peace, May 11, 2017. For a more detailed discussion of al-Azhar, see Nathan J. Brown's "Post-Revolutionary al-Azhar," Carnegie Endowment for International Peace, September 2011. The rise of the Muslim Brotherhood has been chronicled in several fine academic works. One of the best is Carrie Rosefsky Wickham, *The*

Muslim Brotherhood (Princeton, 2013). For a thoughtful discussion of the Brotherhood's brief moment in power and its crushing fall by an analyst living in Egypt at the time, try H.A. Hellyer, *A Revolution Undone* (Oxford, 2016). For an overview of the rise of Salafism in Egypt, see Khalil al-Anani's chapter in *Salafism after the Arab Spring* (Oxford, 2016). Stéphane Lacroix offers an insightful analysis of the political strategy of the largest Salafi party, al-Nur, in "Egypt's Pragmatic Salafis," Carnegie Endowment for International Peace, November 1, 2016. For a concise overview of the radical groups that threaten Egypt's stability, see Hebatalla Taha's chapter in *Egypt after the Spring* (Routledge, 2016) or the essay by Mokhtar Awad and Mostafa Hashem, "Egypt's Escalating Islamist Insurgency," Carnegie Endowment for International Peace, October 21, 2015.

7

FOREIGN AFFAIRS

How Does Geography Shape Egypt's Foreign Policy?

Egyptians consider their country the natural leader of the region in part due to its location at the crossroads of Africa, Europe, and Asia. The completion of the Suez Canal in 1869 reinforced the country's geographic centrality, making it a transit point for commerce between Europe and Asia. Egypt's proximity to the oil states of the Persian Gulf and the size of its military also make it an important contributor to the protection of the region's oil reserves.

Another significant feature of Egypt's geography is its long borders with Libya, Sudan, and Israel. In each case, these borders are distant from the major population centers along the Nile. Furthermore, the local residents who reside in border areas often do not recognize the official boundary. From their standpoint, it is simply a line drawn on a map by some long-forgotten colonial official without any natural typography (such as mountains or rivers) to indicate an actual border. Particularly along the Libyan and Sudanese borders, these local peoples are members of tribes that have branches on both sides of the border and move freely back and forth.

Egypt must maintain sufficient military capability to patrol these borders and, if necessary, deploy more troops to defend them on short notice. It also needs to maintain good relations with its neighbors to facilitate cooperation in controlling the flow of illegal goods, weapons, criminals, and other threats. Egypt must sustain these relations regardless of ideological or policy differences. Similarly, when a neighbor's political system collapses—such as the disintegration of Libya after the removal of Qaddafi in 2011—Egypt's security forces become very concerned about fighters and weapons moving across the border. For example, Egypt has carried out several military operations in eastern Libya in the past few years in order to weaken nonstate actors that it considers threatening. The Egyptian government also built a large military base near the Libyan border.

Finally, as mentioned in Chapter 5, Egypt relies on the Nile for its survival. The Nile's furthest headwaters lie in Rwanda, and the river passes through six other countries on its way to Egypt—Burundi, Tanzania, Kenya, Ethiopia, Uganda, and Sudan. One of the central concerns of Egyptian foreign policy is to ensure sufficient flow of the Nile's waters through these countries to Egypt.

A 1959 treaty governs the allocation of Nile water between Egypt and Sudan. This agreement grants Egypt 55.5 billion cubic meters of Nile water each year, roughly 75 percent of the river's flow at the time of the treaty. The remainder was allocated to Sudan. The other upstream states were not included in the negotiation and did not receive an allocation of water on the grounds that, at the time the treaty was drafted, they were not yet independent countries. As these other countries have grown economically and demographically, they have asserted their right to build dams and irrigation systems on the Nile. A council of Nile basin ministers was established in 1998 to negotiate a new framework for sharing the river's water, but has made little progress.

Egypt insists that the upstream countries enjoy significant rainfall and, thus, have a less urgent need for the Nile's water than rain-starved Egypt. Egyptian officials have focused on finding ways to increase the flow of water in the Nile and its tributaries rather than renegotiate the 1959 treaty. For example, in 1998, Egypt funded a three-year project in Uganda to remove aquatic vegetation that blocked the movement of water from Lake Kyoga into the Nile. Egypt also supported construction of a canal in southern Sudan (the Jonglei Canal) designed to bypass a large swamp, thereby reducing water loss through evaporation. Ongoing violence in southern Sudan prevented this project from moving forward. In addition, international lenders and environmental organizations raised significant concerns about the Jonglei project as it would have drained one of the largest and most biodiverse wetlands in Africa.

In 2011, Ethiopia began construction of the Grand Ethiopian Renaissance Dam on the Nile, creating a new diplomatic and security challenge for Egypt. When Ethiopia begins filling the dam's enormous reservoir in 2018, the Nile's flow will decrease for at least five years and perhaps longer, and then settle to an as-yet-undecided level. By some estimates, the decrease in Nile flow during this period could approach 25 percent, which would dramatically affect Egyptian agriculture and sharply reduce the amount of electricity generated by the Aswan High Dam.[1]

Egypt and Ethiopia have held numerous meetings to discuss these issues but have failed to find common ground. If the two countries can reach agreement, several possibilities for cooperation emerge. For example, Egypt has long kept the Aswan High Dam reservoir, Lake Nasser, at high enough levels to ensure sufficient water in times of drought. Since Ethiopia can now store Nile water, Egypt could reach an agreement with Ethiopia regarding the storage and release of water that would allow Egypt to lower its reservoir in Lake Nasser and thus lose less water to evaporation.

How Does Egypt's Economic Situation Constrain Its Foreign Policy?

As discussed in Chapters 3 and 4, Egypt's economy has deep structural weaknesses. The large and inefficient state-owned sector is not competitive in the global economy and is unable to generate sufficient jobs to employ the country's youth. The government suffers from chronic budget deficits due, in part, to an extensive subsidy system that is unsustainable. In addition, the economy must generate enough foreign exchange to cover payments on foreign loans and the cost of imported food and other essentials. These economic challenges place important constraints on the country's foreign policy. In the near term, it must maintain access to sufficient foreign exchange to meet its needs—whether through increased exports or, more likely, through financial aid from supportive countries. In the medium term, it must acquire the technology, management skill, and capital to restructure its economy and become more globally competitive.

Egypt has accessed short-term financial assistance from the Arab states of the Persian Gulf and from the International Monetary Fund. The Persian Gulf countries also employ roughly 500,000 Egyptians, which helps to alleviate the unemployment problem at home and provides an important source of income for many families. For meeting the medium-term challenges of economic restructuring, the only actors willing to step forward so far have been Europe and the United States and the international economic institutions that they control, namely the World Bank and the IMF.

Egypt has little choice but to expand its exports in order to acquire the foreign exchange needed for imports and debt payments. In addition, it must attract foreign investment, since it lacks sufficient domestic capital to support the growth rates needed to employ its population. Egypt must thus be fully engaged with the global economy, even if some Egyptians are injured by the displacements produced by globalization. These pressures also explain why trade promotion has been a continuing feature of Egypt's foreign policy. The country has tried on several occasions to leverage its strategic importance to gain favorable trade agreements. For example, Egyptian officials have called for a Free Trade Agreement with the United States for over 20 years and continue to assign a high priority to this goal.

For economic reasons, Egypt's policymakers must preserve good relations with the Arab Persian Gulf states, Europe, and the United States as its primary trade and investment partners. China has recently increased its involvement in Egypt through expanded trade and some investments. Chinese construction firms are helping to build a new administrative capital east of Cairo with financing provided by the Chinese government. In addition, Russia has become a more important economic partner through recent agreements for arms sales and the development of nuclear energy.

Which Domestic Constituencies Influence Foreign Policy?

Several domestic actors exert influence over Egypt's foreign policy. The most important include:

Businessmen: Since the mid-1970s, private businessmen with close ties to the state have been important supporters of the regime. Foreign policy decisions that affect the flow of finance or trade significantly impact this constituency. For example, many of Egypt's most successful private businesses rely on financing from businesses and banks in the Persian Gulf states. As a consequence, they often advocate for strengthening and deepening Egypt's ties to Saudi Arabia and other Gulf states.

Military: Egypt's leaders avoid foreign actions that the Egyptian military does not support or that might jeopardize relationships with countries that provide weaponry and military assistance. The military has developed particularly close ties with the United States, which has provided substantial military aid for almost 40 years. An entire generation of officers has been trained and promoted in an environment where the United States was the primary source of the country's weapons and an important advisor on strategic doctrine. This relationship, and the financial rewards that flow from it, have given the military a strong incentive to sustain Egypt's ties with the United States.

Public opinion: While Egypt remains an illiberal regime, public opinion still matters, particularly on sensitive issues in foreign policy. The state exerts considerable efforts to mold public opinion through direct ownership of some media outlets, close relationships with private media barons, censorship laws, and harassment of media outlets that criticize the government. The rise of social media (particularly Facebook, the platform most frequented by Egyptians) has contributed to the fragmentation and polarization of public opinion on a range of issues including relations with other countries. However, most Egyptians continue to rely on television to receive their news. Almost two-thirds of Egyptians report not using the internet at all.[2]

Survey research in the Arab world has improved significantly in recent years and provides valuable insights into public opinion. For example, the 2016 Arab Barometer survey asked Egyptians about the future priorities of the country's foreign policy. Eighty-four percent wanted stronger relations with Saudi Arabia and 50 percent wanted stronger relations with Russia. Only 33 percent and 32 percent respectively thought that better relations with the EU and with the United States were desirable. When asked about the influence of external countries on the development of democracy in Egypt, over half of Egyptians polled (51 percent) said the influence of the United States had been very or somewhat negative. An even stronger majority (62 percent) said that the most positive thing the United States could do in their country was to "not get involved." Another 58 percent said that pressure from outside for reform was unacceptable or harmed the national interest.

What Is the Basis for the Egypt-US Relationship?

This relationship has been driven by pragmatic calculations of self-interest on both sides. For the Americans, the overriding strategic concerns are to ensure the smooth passage of shipping through the Suez Canal, guarantee the security of Israel, and project American power into the Persian Gulf both for preserving the flow of oil and for limiting Iran's influence. Egypt has also been a valuable source of intelligence and security cooperation for confronting radical Islamic groups.

For the Egyptians, the United States provides steady and substantial military assistance that has created one of the best-equipped militaries in the Arab world. This assistance entails direct transfers of military equipment and technology as well as support for the development of Egypt's armaments industry. The United States also supplies some economic assistance, but direct economic aid has declined since the mid-1990s, when the United States shifted its assistance program from "aid to trade." This shift reduced direct US economic assistance in favor of increasing US investment in Egypt and expanding US imports of Egyptian products.

The broad strategic outlines of the Egypt-US relationship have proven remarkably durable. Through the 1979 revolution in Iran, two US-led wars in the Persian Gulf in 1990–1991 and 2003, and several bouts of domestic upheaval in Egypt culminating in Mubarak's removal in 2011, the calculations by both actors have been guided by these core interests. The result has been a sustained, if sometimes rocky, relationship. The United States is, obviously, the more powerful actor. However, Egypt is not without leverage. Its leaders are aware of Egypt's importance to the United States and the enormous costs the United States would face if Egypt were to weaken or terminate the relationship. This awareness has enabled Egypt to resist American pressure on some occasions. The government has criticized American policy toward the Arab-Israeli conflict as biased toward Israel. On occasion, it has taken a harsh stance toward American citizens working in Egypt, particularly those involved in efforts to promote political change. The prominent Egyptian scholar and political activist Saad Eddin Ibrahim—who holds both American and Egyptian citizenship—was imprisoned on flimsy grounds for close to a year in the early 2000s, despite protests from the American government. American NGOs that promote political reform— such as the National Endowment for Democracy—have faced several crackdowns, including prison sentences for Americans who worked for these groups. These examples demonstrate Egypt's room for maneuvering within the relationship as well as the limits on the United States' capacity to advocate for po- litical reform.

Egypt's closeness to the United States carries a political cost. Despite its rhetoric, Egypt had little choice but to accept Israeli policies that received intense criticism elsewhere in the Arab world such as the Israeli invasion of Lebanon in 1982 and the suppression of the Palestinian populations in Gaza and the West Bank. Mubarak's critics often asserted that he had surrendered the country's independence and dignity in order to cultivate close ties to the United States.

When Mubarak was deposed in 2011, his successors announced plans to diversify Egypt's foreign relations. In practice, this entailed a few weapons deals with other coun- tries (particularly France, Britain, and Russia) and some eco- nomic deals with China, particularly infrastructure projects that China offered to fund. Russia has also sought to expand its trade ties, and recently signed an agreement to build Egypt's first nuclear reactor, which will utilize a $25 billion low- interest loan from Russia. Russian firms have also invested in the development of Egypt's oil and gas reserves. However, after nearly four decades of acquiring American weaponry to build the Egyptian military, the country has little choice but to continue a close relationship with the United States. At a minimum, it must have access to the spare parts needed to maintain this military equipment and the technical expertise to service it.

In addition, neither Russia nor China has expressed an in- terest in providing the degree of economic assistance and ad- vice needed to restructure Egypt's economy and integrate it more fully into the global economic system. Egypt's need for economic assistance, technology, management expertise, and markets necessitates sustained engagement with the global economy where the United States plays a leading role. As a consequence, maintaining a strong relationship with the United States is unavoidable—despite the political costs and occasional embarrassment that flows from these ties.

How Has Egypt's Relationship with the United States Developed over the Past 50 Years?

Egypt's relationship with the superpowers has always been a source of both constraints and opportunities. As mentioned in Chapter 3, Nasser developed close ties to the Soviet Union in the 1950s and 1960s. After Egypt's defeat in the 1967 war with Israel, he turned to the Soviets even more decisively for new equipment and training. As part of this support, the Soviets sent 20,000 advisors to assist with rebuilding Egypt's military.

When Sadat assumed power in 1970, he faced great pressure from the Egyptian public and the military to regain the Sinai Peninsula, which had been lost to Israel in the 1967 war. However, he also wanted to end the conflict with Israel, partly because of its strain on Egypt's economy. The constant state of war meant that enormous sums of money were channeled to the military, rather than economic development. The unending conflict also had negative impacts on tourism, Suez Canal tolls, and foreign investment. Sadat was convinced that the United States held the key to brokering peace with Israel. He also believed that only the United States had the resources and expertise to help Egypt's economy grow. Thus, Sadat made the strategic decision early in his administration to reorient Egypt from the Soviet Union to the United States. His expulsion of Soviet advisors in 1972 was, in part, a gesture to the United States that he sought to redirect Egypt toward the West.

Sadat's strategy in the 1973 war with Israel sought to demonstrate to the United States the importance of Egypt for regional stability and, thereby, persuade the United States to invest in a sustained relationship with his country and his re gime. The war ended in a ceasefire between Israel and Egypt that left each country's military deployed throughout the Sinai Peninsula. Both countries were eager to carry out an orderly withdrawal of their troops and avoid unintended clashes that might reignite the war. This diplomatic/military challenge created an opening for the United States. A US delegation, led by Henry Kissinger, mediated the negotiations and facilitated what became known as the Sinai Disengagement Agreements. These negotiations also developed the relationships among political and military leaders on both sides that eventually led to the Camp David peace process, which was facilitated and mediated by US President Jimmy Carter. These negotiations produced a peace treaty between Egypt and Israel in 1979, which was signed at the White House.

Egypt faced sharp criticism in the Arab world for signing the peace treaty. For decades, Arab leaders had presented a unified front to Israel in the belief that this unity would maximize their influence and bargaining power. Sadat's decision to sign a separate peace with Israel withdrew the largest and most powerful Arab state from this unified front. In response, Egypt was ostracized. Most Arab nations severed diplomatic ties and the country was expelled from the Arab League. Financial assistance from the wealthy countries of the Persian Gulf ended.

Partly to offset this cut in Persian Gulf aid, the United States began a program of economic and military assistance that totaled roughly US$2.2 billion annually for the next two decades. The United States still sends substantial aid: in 2015, it sent US$1.3 billion in military assistance and US$150 million in economic assistance. By the end of 2015, the United States had sent over US$76 billion in economic and military assistance to Egypt over the previous 36 years (in dollars not adjusted for inflation). The military assistance package has stayed at roughly US$1.2–1.3 billion per year since the early 1980s. When the impact of inflation is considered, the purchasing power of annual American military aid has fallen substantially. Nonetheless, US military assistance still accounts for roughly one-half of Egypt's annual acquisitions budget for new military equipment.

US military and economic support has been premised on the idea that Egypt is a moderate, pro-Western Arab country whose interests often align with those of the United States. Mubarak took several steps during the 1980s and 1990s that reinforced this idea. He attempted to mediate the Arab-Israeli conflict on several occasions, holding both private and public meetings to bring the parties together. Egypt also played an important role in the 1990–1991 Gulf War. The war began when Iraq under Saddam Hussein invaded Kuwait. At the request of Kuwait and Saudi Arabia, the United States deployed upward of 500,000 troops to expel the Iraqis. Mubarak convened a meeting of the Arab League in Cairo that denounced the invasion and called on Arab countries to send troops to reverse it. Egypt sent over 30,000 soldiers to the war zone. While the United States military did the bulk of the fighting, Egypt played a valuable diplomatic and political role by lending its legitimacy to the military action (Syria did the same). Egypt's participation helped to refute accusations that the war was an American colonial intervention and enabled the United States to portray the conflict as civilized nations confronting a rogue Iraq that had broken international law. As mentioned in Chapter 3, Egypt's participation in the war was rewarded with extensive economic assistance and forgiveness of many of its debts to the United States.

Mubarak adopted a different posture during the US-led invasion of Iraq in 2003. He feared that the invasion would destabilize Iraq and provide an opportunity for the expansion of Iranian influence, and also believed that it would spark widespread public anger that could destabilize Egypt and other countries in the region. He further worried that a large American military intervention would confirm the ideological claims of radical Islamic groups, which asserted that the United States was bent on dividing and dominating the Islamic world. Despite these concerns, Mubarak provided discrete support for the American intervention. Egypt had a long-standing policy of allowing American military ships to pass through the Suez Canal with minimal delays, and permitting American military aircraft to fly over Egyptian territory. Mubarak continued these policies during the Iraq war.

Has the United States Tried to Promote Democracy in Egypt?

Egypt's relationship with the United States expanded in the 1970s under the administration of Jimmy Carter (1977–1981). Carter emphasized the importance of human rights in American foreign policy and raised this issue repeatedly with the Egyptian government. In response, Sadat undertook a limited opening of the political system. He allowed several political parties to compete in parliamentary elections in 1978 and permitted a modest expansion in press freedom. However, he reversed these policies toward the end of his administration and engaged in an extensive crackdown on opponents in the last few months of his rule. These steps made clear that the earlier reforms were largely cosmetic and that the underlying repressive apparatus of Egypt's security state remained in place.

Over the next several decades, the US tried to move Egypt toward a more open political system. These efforts were initially cast as "institutional development" that would yield a more stable and effective state by strengthening political parties, civil society groups, and the judiciary. They received limited but sustained funding from the early 1990s onward. Nonetheless, officials on both sides of the relationship understood that America's core strategic concerns would always outweigh the importance of political reform.

This view was reassessed during the administration of George W. Bush. After the terrorist attacks on the United States on September 11, 2001, Bush argued that terrorism by radical

Islamists was partially a result of the repression and stagnation of Arab dictatorships. In Bush's view, these suffocating conditions produced a large pool of frustrated, hopeless, and angry young men and women who yearned for greater dignity and purpose in their lives. They became easy recruits for terrorist ideologues promising honor and martyrdom in a struggle against injustice. For proponents of this view, the key to defeating terrorism lay in ending repression and poor governance in the Arab world. In a speech in Cairo in June 2005, Secretary of State Condoleezza Rice asserted that "for 60 years the US pursued stability at the expense of democracy . . . in the Middle East and we achieved neither. Now we are taking a different course. We are supporting the democratic aspirations of all people." US officials at all levels called on Egypt to improve its human rights record, increase the independence of the judiciary, allow the emergence of vibrant opposition parties, and permit free and fair elections.

These efforts produced some gestures by the Egyptian government but little substantive change. For example, Mubarak agreed to amend the Egyptian Constitution in 2005 to allow for competitive presidential elections (previously, the president was nominated by Parliament and then confirmed by the people in a referendum). However, the details of the amendment and the supporting laws effectively prevented any opposition candidate from mounting a viable challenge. Mubarak also allowed a relatively free parliamentary election campaign in the fall of 2005, but then reverted to the old tricks of rigging and fraud when it appeared that the Muslim Brotherhood was likely to do well. Following the election, Mubarak embarked on a widespread effort to weaken the Brotherhood by arresting its leaders and confiscating its financial assets. He also initiated a crackdown on opposition journalists, which led to large fines and imprisonment for some critics of the regime. As Mubarak undertook these measures that were clearly at odds with America's goal of building democracy, the United States remained largely silent. Rice visited Egypt again in 2007 and adopted a tone sharply different from her 2005 visit. She made little mention of political reform in either public appearances or press releases.

This shift was due, in part, to the outcome of elections in neighboring Gaza in 2006 that brought Hamas to power. This unexpected result tempered the Bush administration's enthusiasm for democracy. In addition, the United States needed Egypt's help on pressing regional matters, particularly growing instability in Gaza, the deteriorating situation in Iraq, and the expansion of Iranian influence. US officials feared that continued emphasis on political reform would lead to less cooperation on these vital issues. This fear was reinforced by comments from Egyptian officials, who claimed that US democracy promotion efforts constituted unacceptable interference in Egypt's internal affairs.

President Obama initially attempted to set US policy toward Egypt in the broader context of improving relations between the US and the Muslim world. The US-led wars in Afghanistan and Iraq had produced growing criticism and suspicion of the US in many Muslim countries. President Obama traveled to Cairo in early 2009 and announced, "I have come here to seek a new beginning between the United States and Muslims around the world . . . one based upon mutual interest and mutual respect; and one based upon the truth that America and Islam are not exclusive, and need not be in competition. Instead, they overlap, and share common principles—principles of justice and progress; tolerance and the dignity of all human beings." The speech was generally well-received in Egypt.

As the large demonstrations of the Arab spring unfolded in January and February 2011, the Obama administration hoped that a process of internal political change had begun and supported the removal of Hosni Mubarak. After the Supreme Council of the Armed Forces (SCAF) assumed power in February 2011, the United States called for free elections for Parliament and the presidency. The SCAF allowed the elections. The Muslim Brotherhood performed very well and won the presidency and control of both houses of Parliament. The Obama administration attempted to work with the Brotherhood on the grounds that it was chosen through an open and democratic process.

When the Egyptian military intervened in July 2013 to remove the Brotherhood from power, the Obama administration criticized the coup but announced only limited measures in response. Senior officials expressed "deep concern" over the removal of an elected leader and suspended some military assistance. However, this concern was soon displaced by growing worry about the rise of radical Islamic groups in Syria and Iraq as well as the general instability engulfing the Middle East. In this setting, Egypt was a relatively stable country that was prepared to confront radical groups and limit Iran's influence. Concerns over the lack of democracy soon faded, and military aid resumed. Obama, like his predecessors, calculated that America's core strategic interests were more important than facilitating political change in Egypt. The earlier argument put forward by the Bush administration and initially echoed by the Obama administration—that democratic change in Egypt was necessary for long-term stability and that Islamist parties would be part of that democratization process—largely disappeared from American policy. This trend has continued under the Trump administration, which has embraced al-Sisi despite his dismal human rights record.

What Is Egypt's Relationship with Israel?

When Israel was founded in 1948, Egypt joined the rest of the Arab world in rejecting it as a creation of British colonialism. Egypt fought alongside other Arab states against Israel in 1948, 1956, 1967, and 1973. In each of these wars, it supplied many of the front-line troops and suffered a large percentage of the total Arab casualties.

As mentioned earlier, Anwar Sadat made a strategic decision in the early 1970s to strengthen Egypt's relationship with
the United States and seek a peace deal with Israel. Sadat
signed a peace treaty with Israel in 1979 followed by deals to
sell oil and natural gas to Israel as well as agreements to facilitate tourism, agriculture, and trade. The peace treaty between
Egypt and Israel has been honored by both sides but has not
led to warm relations. The Egyptians saw the Camp David
process as a first step toward the establishment of a Palestinian
state and a just solution to the plight of Palestinian refugees.
Instead, Israel took actions regarded by Egyptians and many
other observers as contrary to peace. These included annexing
East Jerusalem in May 1980, annexing the Golan Heights in
December 1981, and building Jewish-only settlements and
roads throughout large portions of the West Bank—all territories occupied during the 1967 war. Israel's invasion of Lebanon
in June 1982 provoked a particularly strong reaction in Egypt.
Many Egyptian commentators argued that Israel was able
to undertake this incursion only because its southern border
with Egypt was calm due to the Camp David accords. Thus,
the Egyptian government was viewed as complicit in this act
of aggression against an Arab state.

These actions led to a freezing of efforts to normalize relations in 1982. The expansion of Israeli settlements in the
occupied Palestinian territories and Israel's harsh handling
of the Palestinian uprising in 1987 fueled further skepticism
about Israel's commitment to peace, and seemed to confirm
the views of those who opposed the strengthening of ties with
Israel. Mubarak publicly criticized the hardships inflicted
on Palestinians. He was also concerned that violence against
Palestinian civilians could ignite public anger in Egypt and
lead to large demonstrations that could threaten the country's
stability.

Mubarak realized that renewed military conflict with Israel
was not an option, as Egypt lacked the military capacity to
defeat Israel. In addition, any military action against Israel

would lead to a sharp reduction in ties with the United States, which would have profound effects on the country's military strength. Furthermore, the economic strain of a war would plunge the country's economy into an even deeper state of crisis. As Egypt's foreign minister, Amr Moussa, noted in 1991, peace with Israel "is no luxury, but a need."[3]

In an effort to alleviate some of the hardships facing Palestinians in Gaza, Egypt allowed greater economic and humanitarian support to cross the Egypt-Gaza border and, in the view of some observers, it turned a blind eye to the tunnels that Gazans and Egyptians dug under the border for smuggling goods, people, and weapons. However, it also periodically destroyed some of the tunnels and constructed a wall to control the border between Gaza and Egypt.

In addition, Mubarak attempted to facilitate a diplomatic solution to the Arab-Israeli conflict. He emphasized that Egypt was the only country that had good relations with the United States, Israel, the Palestinians, and the Arab Persian Gulf countries. As a consequence, it could bring them together around shared interests including the resolution of the conflict. Egyptian officials attempted to mediate throughout the 1980s and 1990s and hosted several meetings of the opposing parties. Mubarak reportedly played an important role in persuading Yasser Arafat of the Palestine Liberation Organization (PLO) to negotiate directly with Israel, which eventually led to the Oslo Peace Accords between Israel and the Palestinians in 1993. Egypt also helped to train the Palestinian security forces, although these forces have engaged in the same sorts of abuses—such as arbitrary detention and torture—that mar the Egyptian security services.

After Arafat's death in 2004, the Palestinian nationalist movement split between Hamas (a Palestinian Islamist movement based in Gaza) and Fatah (Arafat's faction of the PLO). This rivalry peaked in the summer of 2007, when Hamas militias expelled Fatah from the Gaza Strip with substantial loss of life. Egypt's diplomatic and intelligence services attempted to mediate between the two parties and produce a unified Palestinian negotiating position. These efforts were unsuccessful, but Egypt continued to work toward a negotiated resolution between the Israelis and the Palestinians throughout Mubarak's term in office.

When Muhammad Mursi was elected president in June 2012, many observers expected that he would take a harsh stance toward Israel. The Muslim Brotherhood was a longstanding opponent of the Camp David peace process and a vigorous critic of Israel's policies toward the Palestinians. However, Mursi made clear that he would abide by the peace treaty with Israel. He played a constructive role in containing a flare-up in violence between Israel and Hamas in the fall of 2012, which both sides commended.

However, Mursi also felt an obligation to provide greater support to Palestinians under Israeli control, particularly those who resided in Gaza. He allowed greater movement of people and goods across the border between Egypt and Gaza. He also called for greater cooperation and coordination with Hamas as part of a broader effort to improve conditions for Palestinians. He asserted that these steps were consistent with Egypt's humanitarian obligations and its political interests. However, his critics would later point to this increased cooperation with Hamas as evidence of his support for radical Islamic groups. After his removal from office in July 2013, Mursi's contacts with Hamas were cited as evidence of treason and were used to justify his imprisonment.

After Abd al-Fatah al-Sisi's rise to power in 2013, Egypt adopted a much tougher stance toward Hamas. Al-Sisi asserts that Egyptian radical Islamic groups have ideological and operational ties to Hamas and that the increase in violence by radical groups in Sinai is partly due to Hamas support. He destroyed the border tunnels that had been an essential lifeline for Gazans and sharply reduced the movement of goods and people across the border. In addition, he expanded security cooperation with Israel in order to combat radical Islamic groups in Sinai.

In recent years, Egypt and Israel have recognized several shared interests that have led to either explicit cooperation or de facto coordination of their policies. They both seek to contain the expansion of Iranian influence in Iraq, Syria, Lebanon, and Yemen. They also seek to defeat radical Islamic groups such as al-Qaeda and Islamic State, and to weaken Hamas's influence in Gaza. Defeating radical Islamists in Sinai is a high priority for both countries. In addition, they oppose populist Islamist movements such as the Muslim Brotherhood that could become a threat to Egypt's regime and mobilize opposition among Palestinians. Finally, they have shared economic interests. Egypt is an enormous market on Israel's doorstep and has ample supplies of skilled and semi-skilled labor. Israel has technical expertise that could be useful to Egypt in areas such as water desalinization, renewable energy, and high-efficiency irrigation systems. The two countries have increased their trade in natural gas in light of recent discoveries of extensive offshore gas fields in the Mediterranean. In addition, the United States has long sought to "warm" the cold peace between Egypt and Israel by encouraging trade ties. Toward this end, the United States supported Qualified Industrial Zones in Egypt that allow Egyptian goods to be exported to the United States under Israel's free trade agreement with the United States as long as these goods contain 10.5 percent Israeli content.

Under al-Sisi, Egypt has sought a resumption of Israeli-Palestinian negotiations. However, the prospects for reaching a deal that meets minimal Palestinian demands have dimmed since the Trump administration recognized Israel's exclusive claim to Jerusalem and halved US funding to the UN agency that supports Palestinian refugees (UNRWA). In Egyptian popular media, Israel remains a target of frequent criticism. A Member of Parliament who simply had dinner with the Israeli ambassador in 2016 faced harsh criticism and was expelled from the Parliament. Al-Sisi must navigate carefully between this deep public concern over Israeli intentions toward the Palestinians and the equally substantial strategic advantages of coordinating and cooperating with Israel on issues of shared interest.

What Is Egypt's Relationship with Europe?

Egypt's size and location have given it an important role in relations between North Africa and Europe for centuries. This role was strengthened in the latter part of the nineteenth century with the completion of the Suez Canal, which serves as an essential conduit for Europe's trade with Asia and for its supplies of oil from the Persian Gulf. Trade between Egypt and Europe has become increasingly important. In 2016, Europe accounted for roughly 40 percent of Egypt's exports and 34 percent of its imports.

With the rise of radical Islamic groups, Egypt has become an important security partner for Europe. Its intelligence apparatus provides useful information about these groups, and its security services detain potentially threatening individuals. In addition, Egypt is viewed as a relatively stable ally in an increasingly tumultuous region. Preserving this stability has become a central goal, although Europeans have differed over the best approach to achieving it. On some occasions, European officials have argued for strengthening Egypt's authoritarian institutions in order to improve their capacity to maintain order. At other times, Europe's leaders have called for greater rule of law, respect for human rights, and democratization in order to build a more accountable government that will enjoy long-term stability.

Europe also holds a long-standing concern about refugees fleeing from the Middle East. The refugee crisis in Syria that began in 2011 intensified this concern. The Syrian civil war has produced almost 6 million registered refugees as of March 2018, according to the United Nations High Commissioner for Refugees. Approximately 1.5 million of these headed to Europe, which led to the economic strain of providing immediate humanitarian support as well as the medium-term expense of absorbing these populations into Europe. There was also considerable concern among European security officials that some of these refugees might support radical groups or be vulnerable to recruitment by them.

Egypt is not a major transit point for Syrian refugees. However, Europe's leaders want to ensure that the country can limit the flow of other refugees—both Egyptian refugees and refugees from elsewhere in Africa who travel through Egypt. They are eager to facilitate reforms that produce a stable and prosperous Egypt which, in turn, will lead Egyptians to stay in Egypt rather than risk the dangerous journey across the Mediterranean.

For most Europeans, the goal is not to halt the flow of all migrants. Europe has an aging population that will lead to a steady decline in its workforce. It needs large numbers of young workers. Egypt has these workers in abundance and, thus, controlled immigration can be constructive for both sides of the relationship. However, Europeans are acutely aware of the risks of uncontrolled immigration and the possible threats it poses to Europe's economy, security, and identity.

The European Union has made several attempts to adopt a unified foreign policy toward the countries of the southern and eastern Mediterranean that include a central role for Egypt. The first of these was the Euro-Mediterranean partnership, which began with the Barcelona declaration of 1995. It had three core components: political and security cooperation, including a proposal to strengthen protection of human rights and promote democracy; economic assistance and cooperation with the eventual goal of creating a Free Trade Area that included all the countries of the southern Mediterranean; and a social and cultural dialogue that facilitated better understanding between Europe and its southern neighbors. Progress on these broad regional ambitions proved very slow and led, in 2004, to an alternative approach called the European Neighborhood Policy (ENP). The ENP consisted of carefully negotiated proposals for economic and political development customized to each country. The EU negotiated an Action Plan with Egypt but only after long delays due largely to Egypt's reluctance to accept stipulations regarding human rights and political reform. In 2008, European nations made another attempt entitled the Union of the Mediterranean. France initiated this effort in conjunction with Egypt. Under the auspices of the European Union, this initiative attempted to promote regional integration and investment projects in transportation, water, energy, environment, education, and commerce.

These EU efforts have consistently fallen short of their goals. Part of the problem lies in the weakness of the EU's foreign policy institutions. The EU created the equivalent of a foreign minister and a diplomatic core (External Action Service) only in 2010. As a consequence, it is still building the administrative apparatus needed to design and implement coordinated policies toward the Middle East. However, the root of the problem lies in EU member states holding different objectives and priorities with regard to Egypt and the broader Middle East. They differ over a range of issues, including the degree of emphasis to place on political reform and human rights; the amount and type of resources to direct toward economic reform and development; the extent of security and intelligence cooperation; the amount of immigration from the Arab world and how it should be regulated; and whether to support American policies and initiatives in the region, particularly with regard to the Arab-Israeli conflict and Iraq. EU policy has been further hindered by challenges within the EU itself— including the financial crisis of the euro that began in 2009, Britain's vote to withdraw from the EU in 2016, and growing Euroskepticism throughout the Union. These considerations limit the potential for a unified European policy toward Egypt and the other countries of the southern Mediterranean, regardless of the strategic appeal of such a policy.

In the absence of a sustained single European policy, individual European countries have developed their own ties with Egypt. Britain has placed a high priority on relations with Egypt, both for its inherent importance and its value as an interlocutor in the Arab-Israeli conflict and the Arab world. France remains engaged with Egypt for similar reasons and, at times, has attempted to take the lead in developing stronger ties between Europe and the countries of the southern Mediterranean—in part, to offset the more prominent role that Germany plays in expanding ties with new EU members in central Europe. Italy has developed substantial economic interests in Egypt and has become the country's largest export market. For example, Italian firms play a particularly important role in the development of natural gas fields off of Egypt's northern coast. Germany, the economic powerhouse of Europe, has also taken a strong interest in Egypt. Germany's chancellor has met with President al-Sisi several times. Their discussions focused on expanding German investment, increasing trade ties, broadening security cooperation, and managing the flow of migrants.

Recent EU initiatives have focused primarily on the issue of migration, which involves both migrants seeking better economic opportunities and refugees who fear persecution at home. EU representatives attempted to negotiate an agreement in 2017 that would enlist Egypt in a regional migration plan. Under this plan, migrants intercepted at sea would be taken to resettlement centers in Egypt. Egypt declined, and instead called on European countries to expand their economic assistance and investment in Egypt in order to ensure its continued stability.

What Are Egypt's Relations with the Arab Countries of the Persian Gulf?

Egypt's relationship with the Arab Persian Gulf states, particularly Saudi Arabia, has undergone substantial change over the past 60 years. During the Nasser era, Saudi Arabia and Egypt were strong rivals for regional leadership. Nasser advocated a revolutionary agenda that sought to transform the Arab world and its politics. Saudi Arabia, under King Faisal, defended the old order of traditional monarchies and regarded the revolutionary zeal of Nasser and his mobilization of the masses as threats. This rivalry, the "Arab cold war," divided the region throughout the 1960s and contributed to the intensification of the civil war in Yemen that, at its height, led to Egypt deploying 70,000 troops in an effort to remove a Saudi-backed monarch.

Nasser's revolutionary agenda took a severe blow after Egypt's defeat in the 1967 war against Israel and ended with Nasser's death in September 1970. Anwar Sadat succeeded Nasser as president and was eager to turn Egypt's foreign policy in a more pro-Western direction. This change included improving relations with the conservative monarchies of the Persian Gulf, which enjoyed strong connections with the United States.

The goal of strengthening ties with the Gulf states gained even greater priority after the 1973 oil embargo. Saudi Arabia and OPEC initiated the oil embargo in response to US military and logistical support to Israel during the 1973 Arab-Israeli war. OPEC suspended oil sales to the United States and reduced oil production, leading to a rapid increase in the global price of oil. After the embargo ended, Saudi Arabia took the lead in coordinating production levels among many of the world's largest oil producers in order to sustain oil prices at high levels. This effort was largely successful and resulted in an enormous increase in revenues for oil producers—particularly for Saudi Arabia, which has the most extensive oil reserves in the region.

Anwar Sadat wanted to attract some of this Persian Gulf wealth to Egypt. His economic reform policy, the *infitah* (opening), was designed with this goal in mind. In addition, millions of Egyptians began working in the Gulf—from low-skilled construction workers to skilled professionals such as doctors, lawyers, and judges. For much of the 1980s and

1990s, the remittance income sent from expatriate workers in the Gulf to their families back home in Egypt was a larger source of foreign exchange than all of Egypt's trade in goods and services.

Sadat's decision to sign the peace treaty with Israel in 1979 slowed the expansion of these economic ties. All of the Arab Persian Gulf states broke diplomatic relations and ceased economic assistance to Egypt. However, their steadily growing concern over the influence of Iran in the region led them to revise this policy. The Iranian revolution in 1979 challenged both the security and the ideology of the Arab Persian Gulf countries, particularly Saudi Arabia. The leaders of the Iranian revolution made clear that they considered all monarchies un-Islamic. They claimed that popular movements would overthrow the region's monarchs, just as they had with the Shah's monarchy in Iran. In addition, the Iranian revolutionaries espoused Shia Islam, which Saudi Arabia's Wahhabi rulers consider an "impure" version of the faith that must be challenged and contained. In an effort to counterbalance Iran's growing influence in the region, all of the Arab Persian Gulf states restored diplomatic ties with Cairo by 1987.

As Saudi Arabia and other Persian Gulf oil producers (such as Kuwait and the United Arab Emirates (UAE)) became wealthier, they began to coordinate their foreign and security policies more fully within the framework of the Gulf Cooperation Council (GCC), founded in 1981.[4] Egypt assumed an increasingly important place in their thinking about Persian Gulf security. Egypt's role in the Persian Gulf expanded sharply during the first Gulf War (1990–1991), when Iraq under Saddam Hussein invaded Kuwait. Hosni Mubarak denounced Iraq and sent Egyptian troops to help liberate Kuwait. The GCC states showed their appreciation by forgiving US$7 billion in outstanding Egyptian debt. After the war, Egypt offered to participate in a pan-Arab security force that would defend the Gulf in exchange for financial assistance. This force never materialized.

Nonetheless, Egypt's economic ties to the Persian Gulf—particularly to Saudi Arabia—have grown dramatically. Between 1991 and 2011, Saudi exports to and imports from Egypt increased tenfold. By 2009, approximately 2,500 Saudi companies had invested almost US$11 billion in Egypt. In 2009, Egypt also received roughly US$9.5 billion in expatriate remittances from the nearly 1 million Egyptian workers in the Kingdom. In recent years, these employment opportunities for Egyptians have declined due to a fall in oil prices, increased use of migrant workers from South and Southeast Asia, and expanded programs to give jobs to local workers in order to reduce unemployment. Nonetheless, Egypt retains strong economic ties with the GCC states on many levels.

Egypt's relationship with the Persian Gulf underwent another period of tension after the uprising in 2011. The GCC countries watched the removal of Mubarak with great concern. They feared that their citizens might be inspired to participate in similar protests, which could threaten their regimes. In addition, one of the key repercussions of the 2011 uprising was the emergence of the Muslim Brotherhood as a major political actor. By July 2012, it had won control of both houses of Parliament and the presidency in Egypt. Saudi Arabia was particularly troubled by the Brotherhood's ascendancy. In its view, the Brotherhood was a competitor for Islamic leadership in the region. In addition, the Brotherhood called for the democratic election of political leaders and the strengthening of institutions that would hold leaders accountable to the populations that selected them. This conception of Islamic politics grounded in broad popular support was at odds with the traditional monarchies that rule Saudi Arabia and the other GCC states.

When Mursi was removed by Egypt's military in July 2013, the reaction among the GCC states was broadly positive (with the exception of Qatar, the only GCC state that backed Mursi). Barely one week later, Saudi Arabia, the UAE, and Kuwait announced US$12 billion in budgetary aid, central-bank support, and oil products for Egypt. They praised Abd al-Fatah al-Sisi, the defense minister who carried out the military intervention against Mursi. When al-Sisi was elected president in June 2014, the Persian Gulf states (except Qatar) voiced their strong support. Saudi Arabia opened its largest embassy in the world in Cairo in September 2014. Saudi Arabia and the UAE also helped finance a Russian arms deal for Egypt in 2014 worth US$2 billion.

At the heart of the growing relationship between the GCC and Egypt are four interests: limiting Iran's influence in the region; confronting Islamic radicalism, particularly in the form of Islamic State (IS); enhancing Egypt's stability in order to ensure that it avoids the violence and disorder that afflict Libya and Syria; and preventing mass demonstrations that could challenge their regimes.

With regard to containing Iran, Egypt makes several important contributions. It has the largest population in the Arab world and, thus, is key to constructing an effective and durable bloc of Sunni countries. In addition, it has the largest military in the Arab world. Most of its military equipment is supplied by the United States, which also supplies the militaries of Saudi Arabia, the UAE, and Kuwait. Thus, there is the potential for Arab Persian Gulf forces and Egyptian forces to combine their military strength and undertake joint operations. A small example of this potential occurred in 2014, when Egypt and the UAE launched air strikes from Egyptian territory against Islamist rebels in Libya using aircraft that both countries had acquired from the United States. In 2015, Egyptian naval vessels were deployed off the coast of Yemen to assist in the Saudi effort to defeat Iranian-backed Houthi rebels. Egypt also sent 800 ground troops to assist in this conflict, which shows no sign of ending and has created a humanitarian catastrophe inside Yemen. In an effort to institutionalize this Egyptian role in regional security, al-Sisi has proposed a joint Arab force involving Egyptian, Saudi, Jordanian, and UAE soldiers.

The Arab Persian Gulf states continue to send extensive economic assistance to Egypt. From June 2013 to June 2015, Saudi Arabia, the UAE, and Kuwait provided over US$29 billion in oil shipments, cash deposits to Egypt's central bank, and investments. A visit by the king of Saudi Arabia to Egypt in April 2016 reportedly led to 36 agreements worth another US$25 billion, including the establishment of a Saudi investment fund valued at US$16 billion, the creation of a free trade zone between Sinai and Saudi Arabia, and the construction of a bridge connecting Sinai to Saudi Arabia. Saudi Arabia has also reportedly promised Egypt an additional US$20 billion of oil products at concessionary rates from 2016 to 2021, in addition to US$8 billion in investments that include US$1.5 billion designated for the Sinai Peninsula.

Egypt's growing dependence on Saudi Arabia for economic support has led some critics to assert that the country is subservient to the Saudis. This criticism became particularly acute in 2016, when Egypt transferred sovereignty over two small islands—Tiran and Sanafir—to Saudi Arabia during a visit by King Salman to Cairo. This decision sparked the largest demonstrations since 2013, with activists claiming that Egypt had sold its territory in exchange for Saudi aid.

Egypt's stance on the wars in Yemen and Syria has also created some tensions. Saudi Arabia would like greater Egyptian involvement in the conflict in Yemen, while Egypt has been careful to limit its deployment in order to focus its security forces on domestic challenges. Saudi Arabia has also called for the removal of Syria's leader, Bashar al-Asad, while Egypt has supported a more incremental process of change that may leave al-Asad in power. Nonetheless, the core strategic foundations of the relationship remain strong and enduring. Their shared religion, economic interests, and security interests render the Egyptian-Saudi axis one of the most durable in the region.

What Is Egypt's Relationship with Iran?

A discussion of Egypt's relationship with the Persian Gulf would not be complete without considering Iran, the Gulf's most populous country (with 80 million citizens) and its second largest economy (after Saudi Arabia). Ever since the Iranian revolution in 1979, relations have been tense. Egypt broke diplomatic ties with the country after the revolution and has not restored them. Indeed, Iran is the only country in the Middle East where Egypt does not maintain an embassy. There are several reasons for this tension. As mentioned earlier, Iran's leaders called for exporting their revolution throughout the Islamic world. While Iran is Shia and Egypt is Sunni, Egypt's leaders nonetheless took this threat seriously. Under both Mubarak and al-Sisi, Egypt's government claimed that Iran supports Islamic opposition groups in Egypt. When Egypt faced an intensification of violence by radical groups in the late 1980s and early 1990s, Mubarak asserted that Iran had ties to these groups.

When Muhammad Mursi held Egypt's presidency in 2012/2013, he attempted to improve relations. He visited Iran, in order to attend a summit meeting of developing countries that participate in the Nonaligned Movement. The Iranian president made a reciprocal visit to Cairo a few months later. Mursi also invited Iran to participate in a regional plan to resolve the Syrian civil war. When Mursi was removed from office, these efforts were portrayed as part of a long-standing relationship between the Brotherhood and Iran. One of the many lawsuits brought against Mursi asserted that he had conspired with Iran to threaten the security of Egypt.

When al-Sisi came to power in 2013, he quickly expressed his suspicion toward Iran and renewed claims that Iran interferes in Egyptian affairs. While the evidence of Iran's involvement with Egyptian Islamic groups is sketchy at best, Egypt's leaders have consistently feared that it seeks to destabilize the country. Iran's support for Hamas in Gaza, in particular, has been invoked as evidence of its links to radical Sunni groups and, thus, its role in threatening Egypt's security. The tension with Iran is also driven by regional dynamics. Saudi Arabia clearly considers Iran a challenger for regional hegemony and has given the confrontation with Iran high priority in its foreign policy. Egypt's value to Saudi Arabia is based, in part, on its capacity to provide a counterbalance to Iran. Thus, Egypt faces very substantial financial rewards if it sustains an anti-Iranian posture and very few benefits if it alters this position.

The other key relationship in Egyptian foreign policy is with the United States, which has made its opposition to Iran's influence in the region clear. Containing Iran has been an American foreign policy objective for almost 40 years. Egypt benefits immensely from its relationship with the United States and is unlikely to jeopardize it by improving relations with Iran.

Suggested Readings

For well-informed discussions of Egyptian foreign policy, see the
chapter by Ali E. Hillal Dessouki in *The Foreign Policies of Arab States: The Challenge of Globalization. Revised Edition* (American University in Cairo, 2008) and the contribution by Raymond Hinnebusch in *The Foreign Policies of Middle East States: Second Edition* (Lynne Reinner, 2014). For a provocative analysis of Egyptian foreign policy in the Mubarak era, see Nael Shama, *Egyptian Foreign Policy from Mubarak to Morsi: Against the National Interest* (Routledge, 2014). Michael Doran's chapter in *Diplomacy in the Middle East: The International Relations of Regional and Outside Powers* (I.B. Tauris, 2001) offers a thoughtful assessment of the Nasser period. For a broad overview of US-Egypt relations, try Lloyd C. Gardner, *The Road to Tahrir Square: Egypt and the United States from the Rise of Nasser to the Fall of Mubarak* (New Press, 2011). Jason Brownlee, *Democracy Prevention: The Politics of the U.S.-Egyptian Alliance* (Cambridge, 2012), provides a comprehensive and critical review of US-Egypt relations with a particular focus on the lack of democracy promotion. Several thoughtful works on the EU's relations with Egypt include *Relations between the European*

Union and Egypt after 2011: Determinants, Areas of Cooperation, and Prospects (Logus Verlag Berlin, 2015); Rosa Balfour, *Human Rights and Democracy in EU Foreign Policy: The Cases of Ukraine and Egypt* (Routledge, 2012); and Cilja Harders' chapter in *Euro-Mediterranean Relations after the Arab Spring: Persistence in Times of Change* (Ashgate, 2013). For a careful discussion of Egypt's relations with the Arab states of the Persian Gulf, see Robert Mason (ed.), *Egypt and the Gulf: A Renewed Regional Policy Alliance* (Gerlach, 2017).

8

PROSPECTS AND CHALLENGES FOR THE FUTURE

Is Egypt Likely to Democratize?

Democracy is generally understood to have two components: the selection of a country's leadership through competitive elections in which most adults may run for office and vote; and the creation of institutions that constrain state power, render the state accountable to law, and protect the civil and political rights of the public.

The prospects for democracy in Egypt are not bright. The country's civil society groups, which are an essential building block for democracy, face a very challenging environment. A new NGO law, adopted in May 2017, states that the work of any civil society group must "agree with the state's plan, development needs, and priorities." These groups may not engage in activities deemed political by the regime. The government may scrutinize their budgets and freeze them at any time. Persons found in violation of the law face prison sentences. In essence, the law aims to depoliticize civil society and render policy advocacy by civil society groups illegal. Similarly, political parties have little capacity to organize social groups or advocate for their interests. Their activities are tightly monitored and their opportunities to campaign and recruit at the grassroots level are sharply constrained. Parties are expected to support the state and reinforce its authority.

Politicians and parties that challenge official policies face withering criticism in the state-controlled media and may face legal prosecution under laws that criminalize disrespect toward state institutions or the president.

The media are also expected to show support for the state. A new media law adopted in December 2016 creates three regulatory bodies that license and monitor all media platforms in the country. They are empowered to close any media outlet that does not comply with their regulations. Journalists who have written articles critical of the government have faced prosecution on the grounds of "incitement against state institutions" or "inciting protest." By one count, 25 journalists were imprisoned for such violations as of December 2016. The government also periodically blocks independent news websites that it considers too critical of the regime. These and other restrictions on the media led Reporters without Borders to rank Egypt 161 out of 180 countries globally for its lack of press freedom.[1]

In addition, the military is a powerful actor with a questionable commitment to democracy. During discussions of the Egyptian Constitution in 2011, 2012, and 2013, the military leadership called for constitutional clauses that would protect it from civilian scrutiny and empower it to intervene in domestic politics and remove an elected government. The military has also demonstrated very limited support for the protection of civil and political rights. During 2011/2012, when it held both executive and legislative power, more than 12,000 civilians were tried in military courts without a sound legal reason. These courts offer fewer procedural protections to the accused than ordinary courts and no opportunity for appeal to a civilian judge.

The military also has institutional interests that would be threatened by democratization. It currently enjoys considerable autonomy from civilian officials and other state institutions. It has wide-ranging powers to formulate policy, decide on promotions, administer its budget, and handle internal discipline. This autonomy would almost certainly decline in a democracy. Furthermore, retired military officers hold substantial power in Egypt's provinces by serving in posts at all levels including provincial governors, secretaries-general, and assistant secretaries-general. If these posts were filled through competitive elections, the military's political influence at the local level would decline sharply.

Furthermore, Egyptian society contains few strong and effective actors who advocate for democracy. Most Islamists are deeply disillusioned by the democratic process. From their standpoint, they participated in free elections in 2011/2012, won fair and square, and were then removed from office in a military coup that led to wide-ranging repression. In addition, secular liberal parties such as the Wafd, the Free Egyptians, and the Social Democratic Party have shown considerable ambivalence about democratic elections when these elections brought Islamists to power. They have also been unable to organize effectively at the local level. Although these parties call for strengthening civil and political rights and constraining state power, they lack the broad popular support that would give these demands traction.

The al-Sisi government increasingly resembles the Mubarak regime in its manipulation of election results. For example, in the 2015 parliamentary elections, the government changed the electoral rules so that most candidates ran as individuals rather than members of parties, which favored candidates with ties to the dissolved National Democratic Party. It also adopted other rules that sharply limited the opportunities for opposition parties to compete effectively, which led several liberal political parties to boycott the election. Ordinary Egyptians largely sat out the vote. By some estimates, no more than 30 percent of eligible voters participated.[2] The reinvigorated role of the security agencies was also apparent. Much as state security personnel helped foster the anti-Brotherhood movement *Tamarrod*, members of the General Intelligence Agency reportedly helped to create and fund a pro-Sisi parliamentary list of candidates, "For the Love of Egypt," which won all 120 seats allocated to parties.[3]

Finally, the international context creates little pressure for democratization. Egypt's two most important allies—the United States and Saudi Arabia—have indicated that democratization is a low priority. President Trump visited the Middle East in May 2017 and gave speeches and interviews stating that the United States would not pressure the governments of the region regarding their domestic politics. He also offered extensive praise to President al-Sisi, despite Egypt's worsening human rights record. Saudi Arabia, whose monarchy provides few civil or political rights, has fully embraced President al-Sisi and extended substantial economic support to his regime. In addition, the European Union has refrained from meaningful pressure for political reform.

What Are the Prospects for Inclusive Economic Development?

As we have seen throughout this book, achieving economic growth is not the same as achieving inclusive development. The Egyptian economy faces serious structural challenges, a regional environment plagued by war and uncertainty, and an increasingly competitive global marketplace. How can Egyptian firms generate jobs that are stable, reward educational attainment, and provide adequate salaries? Can Egypt diversify into non-hydrocarbon exports and attract foreign investment in more labor-intensive sectors? Will tourism and investment recover given extensive corruption and continuing internal and regional violence? How can small farmers be supported when the state favors large agribusiness? How can the banking system and credit markets serve not only large private and state-owned firms but also small- and medium-sized enterprises essential to innovation and employment? Can backward and forward linkages between large and small firms be fostered to increase employment, reduce dependence on imports, and help small firms to grow? How can Egypt's increasingly educated women join the labor force in greater numbers?

These numerous economic challenges are compounded by political difficulties. Many of the structural changes needed to make Egypt's economy more competitive and efficient impose substantial costs on regime allies and on the general population. A good example is the government's efforts to reduce spending on energy subsidies. In 2013, these subsidies accounted for approximately 22 percent of all government expenditures, more than health and education spending combined. While the better-off segments of Egyptian society consume more energy, and therefore use more fuel than poorer households, paying for energy consumes a larger share of household income for the poor than for the wealthy. As a consequence, cuts in energy subsidies disproportionately affect poorer households. In 2014 and 2015, the al-Sisi government cut subsidies sharply, which led to large price increases for fossil fuels and electricity. To compensate for the negative impacts on vulnerable households, the government increased social spending on education and healthcare and promised better targeting of cash transfer programs to those in need. However, Egypt's social safety net for poor Egyptians is woefully inadequate. Social safety programs met only 10 percent of the consumption needs of the poorest fifth of Egypt's families in 2013.[4] So far, there is little evidence that the new programs for supporting the poor are more effective. Without a stronger social safety net, austerity measures are likely to deepen poverty and raise the likelihood of political instability.

As the government continues to raise prices on basic goods such as fuel and electricity, it will need to direct even more funds into social programs and further improve their effectiveness. These funds could be acquired by scaling back the enormous infrastructure projects discussed in Chapter 1, which often consume vast resources while providing very limited economic benefits. Spending on the military and internal security forces could also be reduced in order to free up funds for social service programs. By one estimate, a 7 percent cut in Egypt's military spending could yield enough funds to halve the number of people classified as poor.[5]

Implementation of many economic reforms—such as establishing a more robust system of taxation, holding the state-owned sector more accountable to market mechanisms, and opening privileged market sectors to more competition—requires political will. Since Egypt opted for a market-based economy in the early 1970s, the country's rulers have failed to strengthen many of the institutions that could support this market orientation. For example, Egypt's enormous bureaucracy would be more of an asset if recruitment to the civil service was more meritocratic and the state paid decent wages to public servants. Similarly, Egypt has a long tradition of a vocal and influential judiciary. Rather than seeking to constrain the judiciary by manipulating the appointment and promotion of judges, the regime and the economy would benefit from strengthening judicial independence and the rule of law.

The economy would also benefit from expanding access to property and credit for small- and medium-sized enterprises. Development economists have long recommended formalizing legal title to informal ("squatter") land and housing. This step would enable the owner of the property to use it as collateral to secure a bank loan, which, in turn, could support the establishment or expansion of a small business. Similarly, small businesses would be aided by much more extensive microcredit programs that give them access to small loans that would enable them to grow.

Civil society organizations and a free media are also important contributors to inclusive economic growth. They are essential for the free exchange of ideas and information that spur economic innovation and growth. However, the Egyptian government continues to tightly monitor and often harass independent unions and other civil society groups. It has also sharply constrained the media through new legislation that expands government monitoring of media outlets and criminalizes reporting that is critical of the government. Sustainable and inclusive economic growth will require a long-term commitment to supporting these and other institutions necessary for a market economy to function.[6]

Lastly, for the government to promote inclusive social development, women's empowerment should be given a more central role in development planning and practice. As we saw in Chapter 4, female education, employment, and other opportunities outside the home improve health outcomes for families, lower fertility rates, and foster economic growth. Women's highly visible participation in the 2011 uprising fostered new discussion and mobilization around women's rights, particularly regarding sexual harassment in public spaces. When women who had suffered harassment and rape started telling their stories on popular TV talk shows and filing court cases, they broke a significant taboo against openly discussing these topics. However, as in many countries including the United States, women's rights and their bodies remain contested politically and socially. Sectarian violence in Egypt has often been triggered by rumors of women's conversions, while Islamist organizations have frequently opposed government legislation to strengthen women's legal rights. To improve the status of women, an array of different actors in Egypt needs to more systematically address gender-based violence, increase access to healthcare and contraception, and tackle obstacles to women's employment.

How Can Egypt Improve the Provision of Public Goods and Services?

Like many countries in the Middle East and North Africa, Egypt has made significant gains over the past half century in raising literacy rates, expanding healthcare, and providing basic services including electricity, water, and sanitation to millions of citizens. As we saw in Chapter 4, progress has also been made on reducing infant and maternal mortality, increasing immunizations, and treating endemic diseases such as bilharzia. Egypt has sharply reduced the number of children who die of preventable causes such as diarrhea by improving water and sanitation systems, distributing simple treatments such as oral rehydration salts, and increasing access to primary healthcare facilities.

The key obstacles to strengthening public services lie in the areas of finance and governance. Although Egypt has rapidly improved access to drinking water and sanitation, for example, utilities and service providers are generally unable to recover the costs of operation and maintenance. This is due largely to the fact that consumer prices for electricity, fuel, and water were set below the costs of providing these goods, as part of the Nasserist social contract for universal subsidies. As a result, public utilities are unable to recover their costs, the quality of services provided declines, and infrastructure deteriorates. Adequate financing for basic services depends in part upon the structural economic reforms discussed earlier. These include revamping taxation systems to make them more progressive and to increase public revenue, and creating adequate regulatory agencies to monitor the quality of public services and safeguard essential natural resources.

The effective delivery of public services also requires government agencies to broaden their reach beyond the capital to the provinces. State agencies need to substantially expand their capacity to engage with local communities, professional organizations, unions, and civil society actors. This broader and deeper engagement at the local level can facilitate the delivery of public services and improve the flows of information required to adequately assess coverage and quality.

As part of this effort, the government needs to redistribute some resources and decision-making from the central ministries in Cairo to Egypt's provinces (governorates) and municipalities. Egyptian cities, for example, have almost no capacity to raise their own revenue or determine expenditures. Instead, centralized ministries in Cairo assess the country's needs at the national level and allocate resources accordingly, often relying on inadequate information and inflexible procedures. The result is long delays and poorly informed decisions that often squander scarce resources on projects that fail to adequately serve the public.

To compound these problems of centralization in development planning, the regime has long subjected professional organizations, unions, and civic organizations to extensive monitoring and frequent persecution. Conflict rather than cooperation continue to mark the regime's relations with these critical service providers. For instance, medical professionals are essential to delivering adequate public healthcare, but the government's relationship with the doctor's union, the Egyptian Medical Syndicate, is often adversarial. After police assaulted two doctors in a Cairo hospital in 2016, doctors staged a large demonstration against police brutality, threatened to go on a selective strike, and offered to provide free public services in all public hospitals. This action followed several previous doctors' strikes protesting low pay, unsanitary conditions, and shortages of medical supplies. In 2015, doctors initiated an online campaign on Facebook to disseminate images of the poor conditions in public hospitals. The photos and videos of unsanitary conditions, trash, and broken equipment quickly spread on social media. The regime responded by criticizing the doctors involved, rather than improving hospital conditions. Egypt's lawyers have faced similar pressures. Even before the doctors mobilized, the lawyers' syndicate had gone on strike to protest the death of a lawyer in police detention. Rather than criminalizing protest, the regime would benefit from working with professional and civic organizations to improve public service delivery.

Public services and environmental protection have long been attractive areas for international donors working in Egypt. These donors are likely to continue their support, due to Egypt's strategic importance. The al-Sisi government will thus be able to draw on outside resources to fund some public

Photo 8.1 Egyptian doctors shout antipolice slogans in front of the headquarters of the Egyptian Medical Syndicate during a protest against police abuse after two doctors were beaten by policemen in a Cairo hospital. The sign shows a police boot stepping on a medical stethoscope and reads "police are thugs."

Cairo, Egypt, February 12, 2016.

Credit: Amr Nabil / AP Photo

investments. The problems with relying on donor funding, however, are significant and well-documented. Their funding is often not well-coordinated and leads to haphazard support for a range of projects, rather than implementation of a clear strategy. In addition, the projects often peter out after donor funding ends. Donor-funded infrastructure, for instance, often relies upon foreign spare parts, technology, and management systems that are not easily available after the project concludes. In addition, reliance on outside aid as a source of budget support dampens incentives to create adequate local systems for financing and fees.

Is Another Mass Uprising Likely?

The uprising in 2011 was rooted in long-standing grievances among the general population regarding abuse by the police and state security, lack of civil and political rights, and deteriorating economic conditions. The catalyst for the uprising was activists calling for public protest combined with a new public perception that large-scale demonstrations could produce meaningful political change. This positive view of the efficacy of demonstrations was due largely to events in Tunisia, where mass protests led to the removal of that country's dictator just a few weeks earlier. Finally, the military permitted the demonstrations to unfold and facilitated Mubarak's departure.

Each of the three broad areas of grievance that led to the 2011 uprising persist and remain significant challenges for the Egyptian government. As discussed earlier, human rights abuses by the security services are a substantial and growing problem. Protection of civil and political rights has been weakened by new legislation that expands the state's surveillance powers, tightens restrictions on NGOs, and limits freedom of expression. The economic situation is also very difficult. Many Egyptians remain in dire economic straits. Inflation rose to over 30 percent in June 2017, while wages have not kept pace, leading to a decline in the standard of living for most Egyptians. The official unemployment rate is over 12 percent and youth unemployment is estimated somewhere above 28 percent. The tourism industry remains dormant due to attacks by militants and the threat of continuing violence. Remittances from Egyptians working abroad have also fallen, due to an economic slowdown in the Gulf.

Despite these pressures, another uprising is unlikely in the near term. Much of the public has a less positive view of street protest than in 2011. The regime and its supporters have engaged in an extensive media campaign to shape the public's perception of the 2011 uprising and, particularly, to link the country's subsequent economic decline and security challenges to this event.

In addition, the government has calculated that its tough stance on terrorism and protest will appeal to many Egyptians who yearn for greater economic stability and personal safety. So far, this calculation has been largely correct. The fear of personal insecurity among Egyptians has declined significantly since al-Sisi took power. In the well-respected Arab Barometer survey, only 19 percent of Egyptians under the Mursi regime in 2013 reported that they felt their security was "ensured or fully ensured." By 2016, 79 percent reported that they felt secure.[7] The survey also found that Egyptians continue to trust the military more than other state institutions. Egyptians are acutely aware of the costly civil wars that unfolded elsewhere in the region after the 2011 uprisings—particularly in Libya, Syria, and Yemen—and many seem prepared to accept a strengthening of the security state in order to avoid such a fate.

The regime has ensured that protest of any kind is very risky. It has sharply increased the penalties associated with dissent and has allowed the security forces to target potential opponents with impunity. Over 1,800 people were forcibly disappeared in 2015 alone, meaning they were abducted, held incommunicado, and usually tortured by security forces before they were released or their bodies appeared. Another 22,000 were imprisoned awaiting trials that same year, prompting the European Parliament to censure Egypt for human rights abuses.[8]

Finally, the military is likely to steadfastly defend the regime rather than support protesters. In 2011, the military had grown distant from President Mubarak and feared that he was engineering a succession to his son that did not fully protect their interests. The generals played a key role in allowing the demonstrations to grow and in orchestrating Mubarak's exit. In contrast, the military in 2018 remains closely tied to President al-Sisi and the regime. Al-Sisi has gone to considerable lengths to expand the military's authority, defend its interests, and allow its economic power to grow. Furthermore, there is not yet a major policy issue—such as succession or economic reform—that divides the military and the president, as was the case in 2011.

For the near-term, then, the regime is likely to endure. It has the repressive capacity to fragment and dominate its opponents and sufficient international support to sustain these capabilities. The regime also has the military behind it to a degree unparalleled since the early years of the Nasser era. The public appears willing to accept the regime's increased use of repression in order to maintain order and avoid the violence that has engulfed Egypt's neighbors. The regime has the added advantage that, at least in the near-term, there is no plausible alternative to al-Sisi. Those who are unhappy with his record are more likely to demand improved performance from the regime rather than rally for its removal.

Economic conditions, however, will remain very difficult for the vast majority of Egypt's citizenry. Inflation continues to outstrip wage growth, job creation is inadequate, and government subsidies for necessities are declining. There is little indication that the political system will liberalize sufficiently to allow for the peaceful expression of the public's growing anger and frustration. As a consequence, the regime is likely to rely on continued repression to maintain order. An optimist might hope that this period of repression will allow for the implementation of difficult economic reforms, followed by a gradual loosening of the grip of security institutions as these reforms begin to bear fruit and the economy starts to grow. However, it is just as likely that the process of economic reform will be managed to favor actors with close ties to the regime and will not generate sufficient jobs to meet the needs of many Egyptians.

A long-term strategy for stability and inclusive growth must pursue several goals. These include opening the political system to peaceful opponents of the regime, including those who once sympathized with the Muslim Brotherhood, thereby reducing the appeal of radical groups. As noted previously, in order to foster economic development, the regime will need to reconsider its spending priorities in order to acquire the funds to invest in health, the environment, and alternative sources of water. Public policies should support family planning and female employment to reduce the rate of population growth. They should also provide credit and financial incentives to support small- and medium-sized enterprises, which are the primary engines of job creation. Social service programs must be better targeted to address abject poverty and the Ministry of Interior reformed to reduce police abuse. The state's capacity to reliably deliver basic services such as education, infrastructure, and medical care also requires dramatic improvement. Toward this end, the government needs to shift at least some political power away from Cairo and allow cities and provinces to raise and spend their own revenue.

The regime's legitimacy is currently grounded primarily in providing security for citizens, implementing large infrastructure projects, and stabilizing the economy through infusions of funds from outside donors. However, the heightened repression that the regime relies upon to maintain order runs the risk of backfiring. Repression without inclusive development and without improvements in human rights is not a long-term recipe for stability.

The heady expectations for a new political and economic order unleashed by the "revolution" of January 25, 2011—as many in Egypt viewed the uprising—have been dashed in the ensuing years. However, public opinion polls indicate that many Egyptians remain positive about their future.[9] The country's long history of national unity and regional importance provides a basis for optimism. In addition, Egyptians have demonstrated remarkable resourcefulness and resilience in the face of economic challenges. They have created informal systems of housing, credit, and employment that sustain much of the population. It remains to be seen whether the current political leadership will allow this ingenuity and resourcefulness to grow and build a more dynamic economy and inclusive polity.

Suggested Readings

For a wide-ranging analysis of the prospects for democracy in Egypt, see Dalia F. Fahmy and Daanish Faruqi (eds.), *Egypt and the Contradictions of Liberalism* (Oneworld, 2017). Robert Springborg's *Egypt* (Polity, 2017) provides an incisive critique of the country's presidential-security system and its toll on economic development since the Nasser period. For insightful discussions of Egypt's military as a political and economic actor, see Zeinab Abul-Magd, *Militarizing the Nation: The Army, Business, and Revolution in Egypt* (Columbia, 2017) and Yezid Sayigh, "Above the State: The Officers' Republic in Egypt," Carnegie Endowment for International Peace, 2012. For a thoughtful discussion of the early years of the al-Sisi regime, see Hazem Kandil, "Sisi's Egypt," *New Left Review* 102 (November–December 2016).

NOTES

Chapter 1

1 Nagat Ali, "The Friday of Rage: The March to Tahrir Square," The Brooklyn Rail: Critical Perspectives on Art, Politics, and Culture, October 4, 2012, http://brooklynrail.org/2012/10/express/the-friday-of-rage-the-march-to-tahrir-square, accessed July 5, 2017.

2 See Ahmed Shokr, "The Eighteen Days of Tahrir," in Jeannie Sowers and Chris Toensing, eds. *The Journey to Tahrir* (London: Verso, 2012), 41–46.

3 Neil Ketchley, *Egypt in a Time of Revolution: Contentious Politics and the Arab Spring* (New York: Cambridge University Press, 2017), 29.

4 The documentary film "The Square," by director Jehane Noujam, follows four Egyptian activists in Tahrir and captures much of the revolutionary spirit of those days.

5 For a thorough discussion of the tensions between Mubarak and the military, see Hazem Kandil, *Soldiers, Spies, and Statesmen: Egypt's Road to Revolt* (London: Verso, 2014), 175–220.

6 Aida Seif al-Dawla, "Torture: A State Policy" in Rabab al-Mahdi and Philip Marfleet, *Egypt: The Moment of Change* (London: Zed Books, 2009), 120–135.

7 For Ghonim's account of the uprising, see his memoir, Wael Ghonim, *Revolution 2.0: The Power of the People Is Greater than the People in Power* (New York: Houghton Mifflin Harcourt, 2012).

8 Ragui Assaad, Caroline Krafft, John Roemer, and Djavad Salehi-Isfahani, "Inequality of Opportunity in Wages and Consumption

in Egypt," *Review of Income and Wealth*. March 2017, https://doi.
org/10.1111/roiw.12289.

9   Ishaac Diwan, "Understanding Revolution in the Middle
East: The Central Role of the Middle Class," *Middle East
Development Journal* 5 (2013), 1–30.

10 Maha Abdelrahman, *Egypt's Long Revolution: Protest Movements
and Uprisings* (London: Routledge, 2015); Mona El-Ghobashy,
"The Praxis of the Egyptian Revolution," *Middle East Report*
258 (Spring 2011), https://www.merip.org/mer/mer258/
praxis-egyptian-revolution.

11 These included the leftist economists Samir Radwan and Gouda
Abdel-Khaleq and the reform-minded judge Mohamed El-
Guindy. The prime minister was Essam Sharif, an engineering
professor and former Minister of Transport who had supported
the protesters in Tahrir.

12 M. Cherif Bassiouni, *Chronicles of the Egyptian Revolution and Its
Aftermath: 2011–2016* (New York: Cambridge University Press,
2016), 60.

13 For a thorough discussion of the 2011/2012 elections that
includes careful analysis of the voting results and polling data,
see Tarek Masoud, *Counting Islam: Religion, Class, and Elections in
Egypt* (New York: Cambridge University Press, 2014).

14 Oxford Business Group, "Improving Productivity: Improving
Agricultural Sustainability and Effectiveness in Egypt," in *The
Report: Egypt, 2016* (London: Oxford Business Group), 241.

15 Kira D. Jumet, *Contesting the Repressive State: Why Ordinary
Egyptians Protested during the Arab Spring* (New York: Oxford
University Press, 2017), 177, 180.

16 Patrik Haenni, "The Reasons for the Muslim Brotherhood's
Failure in Power," in Bernard Rougier and Stephane Lacroix,
eds. *Egypt's Revolutions: Politics, Religion, and Social Movements*
(New York: Palgrave Macmillan, 2016), 30–31.

17 Ben Hubbard and David D. Kirkpatrick, "Sudden Improvements
in Egypt Suggest a Campaign to Undermine Morsi," *New York
Times*, July 10, 2013. Jumet, 156, 160–161.

18 Neil Ketchley, "How Egypt's Generals Used Street Protests
to Stage a Coup," *Washington Post (Monkey Cage blog)*, July 3,
2017. Asma Alsharif and Yasmine Saleh, "Special Report: The
Real Force behind Egypt's 'Revolution of the State,' " *Reuters*,
October 10, 2013. Philip Marfleet, *Egypt: Contested Revolution*
(London: Pluto Press, 2016), 163. Jumet, 186–187.

19   Ketchley, *Egypt in a Time of Revolution*, 115.

20   Ibid., 117.

21   Jumet, 191–195.

22   David Mepham, "Repression Unbound—Egypt under Sisi," Human Rights Watch, November 4, 2015, https://www.hrw. org/news/2015/11/04/repression-unbound-egypt-under-sisi, accessed August 18, 2017.

23   Ketchley, *Egypt in a Time of Revolution*, chapter 6.

24   Declan Walsh and Nour Youssef, "For as Little as $3 a Vote, Egyptians Trudge to Election Stations," *New York Times*, March 27, 2018.

25   Amnesty International, *Egypt: Officially, You Do Not Exist: Disappeared and Tortured in the Name of Counter-Terrorism* (London: Amnesty International, July 12, 2016). "Report of the Working Group on Enforced or Involuntary Disappearances," United Nations Human Rights Council, July 28, 2016, 15.

26   Central Bank of Egypt, Monthly Statistical Bulletin, November 2017, 14–15, 17. http://www.cbe.org.eg/en/EconomicResearch/ Publications/Pages/MonthlyStatisticaclBulletin.aspx, accessed March 15, 2017.

27   Jeannie L. Sowers, "Re-mapping the Nation, Critiquing the State: Environmental Narratives and Desert Land Reclamation in Egypt," in Diana K. Davis and Edmund Burke III, eds. *Environmental Imaginaries in the Middle East: History, Policy, Power, and Practice* (Athens: Ohio University Press, 2011), 158–191.

28   Hazem Kandil, "Sisi's Egypt," *New Left Review* 102 (November/ December 2016), 21.

29   Hoda El Nemr and Ahmed Ashour, *Egypt's Progress towards Millennium Development Goals* (New York: United Nations Development Programme (UNDP) and the Ministry of Planning, Monitoring and Administrative Reform, 2015), 8. http://www. eg.undp.org/content/dam/egypt/docs/Publications/Docs%20 MDGs/Final%20MDG%20English%202015.pdf, accessed June 15, 2017.

Chapter 2

1   Afaf Lutfi al-Sayyid Marsot, *A Short History of Modern Egypt* (New York: Cambridge University Press, 1985), 71–72.

Chapter 3

1 Hazem Kandil, *Soldiers, Spies, and Statesmen: Egypt's Road to Revolt* (London: Verso, 2012), 8.

2 John Waterbury, *The Egypt of Nasser and Sadat: The Political Economy of Two Regimes* (Princeton, NJ: Princeton University Press, 1983), 66–79, 243; Khalid Ikram, *The Egyptian Economy, 1952–2000: Performance, Policies, and Issues* (New York: Routledge, 2006), 92, 155.

3 Ikram, 160, 171, 172, 158.

4 Ibid., 243. Nazih Ayubi, *Bureaucracy and Politics in Contemporary Egypt* (London: Ithaca Press, 1980), 157–187, 243, 94; Waterbury, *The Egypt of Nasser and Sadat*, 242, 243.

5 Ikram, 24–26, 92, 155, 158.

6 Ibid., 55, 56, 58.

7 Ibid., 78.

8 Howard Handy, *Egypt: Beyond Stabilization: Toward a Dynamic Market Economy* (Washington, DC: International Monetary Fund, 1998), 52.

9 Kandil, *Soldiers, Spies, and Statesman*, 123–139.

10 Ibid., 168–169.

11 Ibid., 169–170.

12 Ibid., 171–174.

13 Ibid., 193–195.

14 Ibid., 195–198.

15 For further discussion of the military's economic power and privileges, see Zeinab Abul-Magd, *Militarizing the Nation: The Army, Business, and Revolution in Egypt* (New York: Columbia University Press, 2017), chapters 3 and 4.

16 Blaydes, *Elections and Distributive Politics in Mubarak's Egypt*, 2, 4–5, 9, 10. Also, Jason Brownlee, *Authoritarianism in an Age of Democratization* (New York: Cambridge University Press, 2007), 124–155.

Chapter 4

1 The UNDP's Human Development Index has been refined with the addition of an inequality-adjusted Human Development Index, a Gender Development Index in 2010, a Gender Inequality Index in 2014, and a Multidimensional Poverty Index. These indices more accurately capture vulnerabilities and limited capabilities among different segments of the population.

2   See http://hdr.undp.org/en/countries/profiles/EGY, last
     accessed July 6, 2018.

3   "27.8 Percent of Egyptian Population Lives below Poverty
     Line: CAPMAS," *Egypt Independent*, July 27, 2016, http://www.
     egyptindependent.com/278-percent-egyptian-population-lives-
     below-poverty-line-capmas/, accessed June 15, 2017.

4   World Food Programme, *The Status of Poverty and Food Security in
     Egypt: Analysis and Policy Recommendations* (Cairo: May 2013), 14.
     http://documents.wfp.org/stellent/groups/public/documents/
     ena/wfp257467.pdf. Accessed July 6, 2018.

5   Ellis Goldberg, *Trade, Reputation and Child Labor in Twentieth
     Century Egypt* (New York: Palgrave MacMillan, 2004).

6   For current population figures, check the population counter at
     the homepage of Egypt's Central Agency for Public Mobilization
     and Statistics, http://www.capmas.gov.eg/HomePage.aspx

7   Egyptian Center for Public Opinion Research (Baseera),
     Population Situation Analysis: Egypt 2016, 23. (Cairo: Baseera,
     National Population Council, and UNFPA, 2016), http://
     egypt.unfpa.org/sites/default/files/pub-pdf/Population%20
     Situation%20Analysis%20WEB%20May23rd.pdf, accessed July 6,
     2018.

8   *Understanding Masculinities: Results from the International Men
     and Gender Equality Survey: Middle East (IMAGES)*, 55. https://
     promundoglobal.org/wp-content/uploads/2017/05/IMAGES-
     MENA-Multi-Country-Report-EN-16May2017-web.pdf.
     Accessed July 6, 2018.

9   http://reports.weforum.org/global-gender-gap-report-2016/
     economies/#economy=EGY, last accessed July 6, 2018.

10   Rana Hendy, *Women's Participation in the Egyptian Labour
     Market: 1998–2012*. Economic Research Forum, Working
     Paper No. 907 (May 2015), 3. https://erf.org.eg/wp-content/
     uploads/2015/12/907.pdf. Accessed July 6, 2018.

11   UN-Promundo, *Understanding Masculinities*, 50. In some
     instances, attitudes toward women's public roles and rights
     converge. Over 93 percent of men and 97 percent of women
     agreed or strongly agreed that women should have the right
     to vote, and 77 percent of men and 89 percent of women held
     that, with the same qualifications, a woman can do as good a job
     as a man.

12   Egyptian Center for Public Opinion Research (Baseera),
     Population Situation Analysis: Egypt 2016, 3. http://egypt.unfpa.

org/sites/default/files/pub-pdf/Population%20Situation%20
Analysis%20WEB%20May23rd.pdf, accessed July 6, 2018.

13 World Health Organization, *Egypt: WHO Statistical Profile*,
http://www.who.int/gho/countries/egy.pdf?ua=1, accessed
July 1, 2017.

14 Human Rights Watch, "UN: WHO Condemns 'Virginity
Tests': Degrading, Discriminatory, Unscientific Procedure Should
Be Banned," https://www.hrw.org/news/2014/12/01/un-who-
condemns-virginity-tests, accessed August 2017.

15 United Nations Human Development Programme, *Arab Human
Development Report 2016: Youth and the Prospects for Human
Development* (New York/Beirut: UNDP, 2016), 78.

16 Hendy, *Women's Participation*, 4.

17 Diane Singerman, "Youth, Gender, and Dignity in the Egyptian
Uprising," *Journal of Middle East Women's Studies* 9:3 (Fall 2013), 10.

18 Ibid., 9–10.

19 Arab Human Development Report 2016: Youth and the Prospects
for Human Development in a Changing Reality," United Nations
Development Programme (UNDP), Nov. 29, 2016, 32.

20 See Tabea Dietrich, Amr Elshawarby, and Tobias Lechtenfeld,
*Egypt's Youth outside Work and Education. MENA Knowledge and
Learning Quick Notes Series. No. 162* (Washington, DC: The World
Bank, 2016). https://openknowledge.worldbank.org/bitstream/
handle/10986/25784/BRI-MENA-Knowledge-Notes-series-
PUBLIC-QN-162.pdf?sequence=1&isAllowed=y. Accessed July 6,
2018.

21 David Sims, *Understanding Cairo: The Logic of a City Out of Control*
(Cairo: American University in Cairo Press, 2010.)

22 Ibid., 31.

23 Ibid., 186–192.

24 Nasser Rabat, "A Brief History of Green Space in Cairo," in
Stefano Bianca and Philip Jodidio, eds. *Cairo: Revitalising a
Historic Metropolis* (Turin: Umberto Allemandi & C. for Aga Khan
Trust for Culture, 2004), 43–53.
https://archnet.org/system/publications/contents/4837/
original/DPC1549.pdf?1384786911, accessed May 20, 2017.

25 Sims, *Understanding Cairo*, 261.

26 Ragui Assaad, Caroline Krafft, John Roemer, and Djavad Salehi-
Isfahani, "Inequality of Opportunity in Educational Attainment
in the Middle East and North Africa," Economic Research Forum,

Working Paper No. 834 (2014), https://erf.org.eg/wp-content/uploads/2014/07/004.pdf, accessed June 2, 2017.

27 The World Bank, https://data.worldbank.org/indicator/per_si_allsi.cov_pop_tot, accessed March 2018.

28 J. Silva, V. Levin, and M. Morgandi, *Inclusion and Resilience: The Way Forward for Social Safety Nets in the Middle East and North Africa* (Washington, DC: World Bank, 2013), 9.

Chapter 5

1 "44.8% of Egyptians Dump Garbage in Street: CAPMAS," *al-Masry al-Youm*, August 15, 2017, http://www.egyptindependent.com/44-8-egyptians-dump-garbage-street-capmas/, accessed August 15, 2017.

2 The World Bank Group and Institute for Health Metrics and Evaluation, University of Washington-Seattle, http://documents.worldbank.org/curated/en/781521473177013155/pdf/108141-REVISED-Cost-of-PollutionWebCORRECTEDfile.pdf, 2016, 28, 94, accessed March 13, 2017.

3 "Water Resources Per Capita Drop 60% since 1970," *Mada Masr*, May 21, 2014, https://www.madamasr.com/en/2014/05/21/news/u/water-resources-per-capita-drop-60-percent-since-1970, accessed July 15, 2017.

4 Amr Adly, "Egypt's Oil Dependency and Political Discontent," Carnegie Middle East Center, August 2, 2016, http://carnegie-mec.org/2016/08/02/egypt-s-oil-dependency-and-political-discontent-pub-64224, accessed July 31, 2017.

5 Justin Dargin, "After the Revolution, Reform," *Petroleum Economist* 81:3 (April 2014), 26.

Chapter 6

1 Hasan al-Banna, "Our Constitution" in Hasan al-Banna, ed. *Collection of the Letters of the Martyred Imam Hasan al-Banna* (in Arabic) (Cairo: Dar al-Nashr al-Islami, n.d.), 35.

2 *Basic Organizational Law of the Muslim Brotherhood* (in Arabic). (Cairo: Dar al-Ansar, 1945).

3 See *Collection of the Letters of the Martyred Imam Hasan al-Banna* (in Arabic), 120–174.

4 Mokhtar Awad, "Why ISIS Declared War on Egypt's Christians," *The Atlantic*, April 9, 2017.

Chapter 7

1 Jean-Daniel Stanley and Pablo L. Clemente, "Increased Land Subsidence and Sea-Level Rise are Submerging Egypt's Nile Delta Coastal Margin, " *GSA Today* (Geological Society of America), 27:5 (May 2017). doi: 10.1130/GSATG312A.1.

2 Daniel Tavana, Egypt: Five Years after the Uprisings. The Arab Barometer, Egypt Wave 4 Country Report, July 20, 2017, http://www.arabbarometer.org/report/egypt, accessed March 8, 2018.

3 Quoted in Nael Shama, *Egyptian Foreign Policy from Mubarak to Morsi: Against the National Interest* (New York: Routledge, 2014), 173.

4 The GCC consists of six countries: Saudi Arabia, Kuwait, UAE, Qatar, Bahrain, and Oman.

Chapter 8

1 Justin Shilad, "As Egypt-US Relationship Moves Forward, Jailed Egyptian Journalists Left Behind," Committee to Protect Journalists, https://cpj.org/blog/2017/03/as-egypt-us-relationship-moves-forward-jailed-egyp.php, March 30, 2017, accessed March 22, 2018.

2 David D. Kirkpatrick, "Low Voter Turnout Reflects System by Design in Egypt," *New York Times*, October 19, 2015, https://www.nytimes.com/2015/10/20/world/middleeast/low-voter-turnout-reflects-system-by-design-in-egypt.html, accessed March 22, 2018. International Foundation for Electoral Systems (IFES), *Election Guide, Egypt*. http://www.electionguide.org/. Accessed June 20, 2018.

3 Hossam Bahgat, "Anatomy of an Election," *Mada Masr*, March 14, 2016, https://www.madamasr.com/en/2016/03/14/feature/politics/anatomy-of-an-election/, accessed July 13, 2017.

4 The World Bank, "Energy Subsidy Reform Facility: Country Brief Egypt," http://documents.worldbank.org/curated/en/873871506492500301/pdf/120075-WP-PUBLIC-26-9-2017-12-41-5-FINALESMAPCountryBriefEgypt.pdf (Washington, DC: World Bank), accessed March 21, 2018.

5 This figure appears in the appendix of the following article: A. El-Zein, J. DeJong, P. Fargues, N. Salti N, A. Hanieh, and H. Lackner, "Who's been left behind? Why sustainable development goals fail the Arab world," www.thelancet.com. Published online January 16, 2016, http://dx.doi.org/10.1016/S0140-6736(15)01312-4.

6 For further discussion of the importance of the free flow of information to economic development, see Robert Springborg, *Egypt,* chapter 6.

7 Daniel Tavana, "Egypt Five Years after the Uprisings: Report from the Arab Barometer," Egypt Wave 4 Country Report, July 20, 2017.

8 Robert Trafford and Mays Ramadhani, "Ruling by Fear: Egyptian Government 'Disappears' 1,840 People in Just 12 Months," *The Independent,* March 10, 2016, http://www.independent.co.uk/news/world/africa/egyptian-government-disappears-1840-people-in-just-12-months-ruling-by-fear-a6923671.html, accessed August 1, 2017. Also, Amnesty International, *Egypt: Officially, You Do Not Exist: Disappeared and Tortured in the Name of Counter-Terrorism* (London: Amnesty International, July 12, 2016). "Report of the Working Group on Enforced or Involuntary Disappearances," United Nations Human Rights Council, July 28, 2016, 15.

9 Tavana, "Egypt Five Years after the Uprising."

INDEX

Figures are indicated by an italic *f* following the page number.